I0460050

Widow Goals

Steps to Finding Peace When You Lose Your Spouse
Michelle Bader Ebersole

MBE Publishing

Copyright © 2025 Michelle Bader Ebersole
All rights reserved.

No part of this publication may be reproduced, distributed, or transmitted in any form or by any means—electronic, mechanical, photocopying, recording, or otherwise—without the prior written permission of the author, except in the case of brief quotations used in book reviews or other non-commercial purposes as permitted by copyright law.

Paperback - 979-8-9987889-0-1

Scripture Acknowledgments:
Scripture quotations are taken from the following versions:

- **Holy Bible, New International Version®, NIV®**. Copyright ©1973, 1978, 1984, 2011 by **Biblica, Inc.®** Used by permission. All rights reserved worldwide.

- **Holy Bible, New Living Translation**. Copyright ©1996, 2004, 2015 by **Tyndale House Foundation**. Used by permission of Tyndale House Publishers, Inc., Carol Stream, Illinois 60188. All rights reserved.

- **The Holy Bible, English Standard Version® (ESV®)**. Copyright ©2001 by **Crossway**, a publishing ministry of Good News Publishers. Used by permission. All rights reserved.

For more resources, speaking inquiries, or to join the Widow Goals community, visit: www.widowgoals.org

Printed in the United States of America
First Edition: May 2025

Contents

Dedication

For Luke, my first great love, who entered heaven on May 23, 2020. Thank you for 17 beautiful years of marriage and for the gift of our three amazing kids. I will never forget your love for us or your unwavering faith in God. You continue to inspire me every day. I love you, always.

And for Joel, my husband and best friend on this new journey. Thank you for believing in me, loving me, supporting me, and understanding the heart of a widow. I love the fun and adventure you bring to my life! Thank you for making me a better person. I love you, always.

Foreword

Heartache is real. Until my husband died suddenly, I thought it was just an expression. Silly, naive, sheltered little me. I had no idea the depth of despair—the deepest pit, the darkest hole—that grief is.

How I long for the "old me" that was blissfully unaware of such tragedy and pain. I would give anything to live in the "before" again. You and I, my friend, are members of the same club. I'm sorry.

Grievers are we. We carry this myriad of emotions and turmoil everywhere we go. It all has a permanent home with us, like it or not. But we are still living. We can carry this grief, carry this love for our person who has departed this Earth too soon, and still thrive.

We can reach out for help, lend a hand to a fellow griever (even if we feel we have nothing to give), smile again, hope again, and allow Jesus to heal us.

What does this healing entail? That probably looks different for all of us. But this book will feel like a warm hug and a gentle nudge forward on your healing and grief journey—from a trusted friend.

Michelle is real, raw, and speaks of nothing she hasn't experienced herself. She's in our club, too. She knows the pain—the utter devastation—that losing a spouse causes.

I lost my husband, Chad, a day before my 47th birthday. He was involved in an auto collision, and I got the phone call that everyone dreads... the call that changes everything about your life in an instant.

Shock, agony, darkness, apathy, depression, anxiety, lack of will to live—all of the swirling thoughts and emotions hit you with the impact of a tsunami.

The hardest thing to handle for me was that I felt so alone. No one in my close group of family and friends had experienced such an out-of-order death like this. I was surrounded by people who wanted to help and were grieving as well, but I felt so disconnected and abandoned.

Nothing felt the same. Nothing about my life was the same. My "normal," happy, boring life was gone, and I was in a new, scary world with no one to help.

This, my friends, is when—at absolute rock bottom—I started listening to the *Widowed 2 Soon* podcast. There was a glimmer of camaraderie. I was hearing someone speak about the exact things I was feeling and didn't even know how to put words to.

I smiled a little every once in a while. I even laughed occasionally.

Is it possible that there are other people navigating this grief journey like me—and they are forging ahead on this path and able to really live again?

YES.

Through the podcast, Grief Recovery, and Widow Goals, Michelle has been a source of comfort, familiarity, hope, and strength for me. She—and this book—can provide the same for you.

There is no checklist to complete your grief journey. Your grief journey is unique, just like your relationship with your person.

I was widowed on June 9, 2023, and initially attempted to conquer grief with sheer will and might. Spoiler alert—that doesn't work!

Michelle and this book have helped me carry grief, respect grief, honor Chad, honor myself, and move forward. Never forgetting. Never dismissing. Just making room for joy, purpose, and little seeds of happiness to be planted. *Widow Goals: Steps to Finding Peace When You Lose Your Spouse* can do the same for you.

Your life is not over, my friend. And you are not alone.

— Kim Lentz, Widow, Grief Warrior, and Sister in Christ

Prologue

May 23, 2020

I woke up to the hallway light flicking on. Startled, I glanced at the clock. It read 4:15 a.m. I reached for my glasses and saw Luke, my husband, standing by the closet, looking for medicine.

"What's wrong?" I asked, my voice quick and concerned.

"My calf really hurts. Can you get me some Tylenol and the heating pad?"

I jumped out of bed and ran to the living room. I plugged in the heating pad, gently placed it on his calf, and handed him the medicine. A few minutes later, he said, "Let's try ice now."

I pushed down the rising fear inside me. I didn't want to consider what might really be going on. I filled a Ziplock bag with ice and returned to his side, placing it carefully on his leg. I stroked his arm and silently prayed.

"I'm getting really worried. My foot is starting to go numb," Luke said, panic rising in his voice. He was usually calm, so I knew something was terribly wrong.

I sprang into action and called hospice. As the phone rang, his breathing started to quicken.

"Lorazepam..." he gasped.

I found the orange bottle marked *Lorazepam* and placed a pill under his tongue. His breathing continued to escalate. I told the hospice nurse on the line, "I called because of his leg, but now he's not breathing well. What do I do?"

"Put the oxygen on him," he said.

I raced to get the machine and slid the tubing into Luke's nose. His rapid breathing slowed, and he said weakly, "That wasn't fun."

I still thought maybe it was a panic attack—something triggered by pain. But then it started again.

And then... his eyes.

His beautiful brown eyes rolled back in his head. That image still wakes me up at night. It haunts me because *that* was the moment I knew. That was the moment everything changed. Until then, I didn't believe he was dying. We'd survived so many close calls: the blood transfusion, the bloating and yellowing, his first bout with cancer, the dangerously high blood sugar, and so much more. So many brushes with death—and every time, he came back. But not this time.

"Should I wake up the kids?" I asked the nurse, panic in my voice.

"I think so," he replied.

I ran through the hallway and into each of my children's rooms. "I think it's time to say goodbye to Daddy," I said gently.

Hayley immediately burst into tears. "No, no—it's not time yet!"

"I'm so sorry," I said. "But I think it is."

They rushed to our bedroom and climbed onto the bed with Luke. His eyes stared blankly at the ceiling. I told them, "Talk to him. He can hear you."

Through tears, we all sang *Jesus Loves Me* as the kids held his hands and told him how much they loved him. I called his mom and my mom and told them to come quickly.

Luke's mom arrived and began singing over him. Luke tried to speak, forming the word "I..." but couldn't get more out. I told him, "It's okay—we know you love us." Later, Hayden had a dream in which Luke came back and confirmed that *I love you* was what he had been trying to say.

Hayley sang *You Are My Sunshine* through her tears. And in that moment, God gave me an unexplainable peace.

"You're going to meet my grandparents today... and see yours," I whispered to Luke.

Then, "Well done, my good and faithful servant."

I called Luke's regular hospice nurse, even though she was off duty. She answered at 5:15 a.m. Later, she told me that God had woken her at 4:00 a.m., and she just *knew* it was Luke's day to go to heaven.

She asked to FaceTime, took one look, and said, "Yes... he's going. Give him the Haldol. It will help him go peacefully."

With Hayley's help, I gently lifted his head and gave him the liquid medicine. I later learned the kids thought it would help him *live*.

Not long after, his eyes turned up and to the right—and stayed there.

"Are you seeing angels?" I asked.

God would later reveal to me in a vision that Luke was looking at Jesus, waiting in the corner of our room.

Something stirred inside me—I grabbed my phone and played *I Can Only Imagine*. Our whole family began singing, and in that sacred moment, Luke took his final breath.

I now know, with complete certainty, that he heard us sing. He felt no pain. He wasn't afraid or sad. He saw Jesus reach out His hand and invite him home—and Luke followed Him into glory.

The nurse arrived, listened to his chest, and gently said, "I'm sorry, he's no longer with us."

And just like that, our lives changed forever.

My babies cried for their daddy. I watched them kiss his cooling face, then quietly leave the room. I climbed into bed beside him, held his cold hand, and looked at the shell of the man I called my husband.

I wailed. A sound from the deepest part of me—a brokenness I didn't know existed. My mom sat beside me and we cried together.

Eventually, she said it was time to go. I just wanted to leave before the coroner arrived—before my kids saw something they couldn't unsee.

I called my best friend from Idaho. We drove to my brother's house. Most of that day is a blur.

But I will never forget walking back into the house and feeling that emptiness.

His prosthetic leg still lay beside the bed. The heating pad was still warm. The ice had melted into a puddle on the floor.

I collapsed next to it. All my strength was gone.

Luke had fought the good fight. He gave everything to stay with us as long as he could.

And now... my husband was in heaven.

And I was left here, in this broken, painful world, trying to figure out how to live again.

Looking back on that day, I now see it as the most sacred—and the most devastating—moment of my life. I watched my husband take his final breath, surrounded by love, music, and the presence of God. I didn't feel ready. I didn't feel strong. But God met me there.

I share this story with you not to retraumatize or overwhelm, but to honor the truth: this part of the journey matters. If you've lived through something similar, I hope you know—you are not alone. If you didn't get a peaceful goodbye, that doesn't mean your spouse didn't feel your love. I truly believe God bridges the gap between earth and heaven in ways we'll never fully understand.

You may be at the beginning of your grief, or this may have happened years ago. But you carry something sacred, too. That final moment, that last word, that last breath—it's part of your story now. You are still here. Still standing. Still breathing.

And that means God isn't done with you yet.

Introduction

Welcome to Widow Goals

If you're holding this book, chances are your heart is broken—and your world has changed in ways you never imagined. First, I want to say: I am so sorry for your loss. I see you. I understand this pain, because I've lived it too.

Maybe right now, you feel completely lost—like you're walking through a fog with no map, no compass, and no idea how to take the next step. I've been there. And I want you to know: you're not alone.

In *Widow Goals*, I'm going to share the small, life-giving goals that helped me survive—and eventually begin to thrive—after the loss of my husband. I've now been widowed for almost five years, and I've learned so much—not only from my own journey, but from walking through grief alongside hundreds of others.

You'll hear me refer to "widows" throughout this book, but please know that when I say widows, I mean widowers too. I see you, men. You are not forgotten. Your pain is real, and this book is for you as well.

Over the past several years, I've worked as a Certified Grief Recovery Specialist, spoken at grief retreats nationwide, and hosted the *Widowed 2 Soon* podcast—where I've had the privilege of holding space for powerful stories of healing and hope. My passion is to be a safe and honest companion for you on this journey.

You can read this book straight through or read any chapter that you want in any order, pausing when you need to. Some days you might just sit with one goal for a while—and that's okay. This is your story, your pace, your healing process. I'm simply here to walk beside you and gently point you toward the One who helped me find my joy again: Jesus.

This isn't a magic formula or a checklist to fix your grief. It's a collection of thirty small but mighty goals that helped me get out of bed, breathe again, and slowly rebuild a life I didn't choose—but one I now live with purpose.

More than anything, I want you to know this: You can survive. You can heal. And yes—you can laugh again. There will come a day when you feel the warmth of the sun on your face and realize... you're starting to live again.

As Philippians 4:7 (NIV) reminds us: "*And the peace of God, which transcends all understanding, will guard your hearts and your minds in Christ Jesus.*"

That kind of peace is possible. Let's take the first step together!

Goal #1–Get Out of Bed

"The steadfast love of the LORD never ceases; his mercies never come to an end; they are new every morning; great is your faithfulness." Lamentations 3:22–23 ESV

I woke up the morning after my husband passed away in utter agony as, suddenly, the memories of his last breath and the sounds of my kids crying out, "No, Daddy, it's not time!" came flooding into my mind. I began to wail because the pain was too intense for me to keep inside. It just couldn't be true. My husband of almost seventeen years couldn't be gone. The father of my children could not have been taken away from them so soon. Even though I had witnessed his death with my eyes, my mind couldn't comprehend it.

The crushing weight of it all was too much to bear. I rolled over and looked at my daughter. The tears flowed more intensely as the harsh reality set in that my daughter, at fourteen, was fatherless. All I wanted to do was go back to sleep to escape the nightmare of my reality. With the sounds of my cries, both of my sisters-in-law came running to my room.

"I'm so sorry, Shell," Jessica said, rubbing my back as I lay face down with my head on the pillow. I could feel the bed shake as my daughter cried by my side. My sweet baby, crying the tears of a broken heart, the tears for her daddy, the tears too deep to be explained. The years of father-daughter dances and dates would now be a bittersweet memory of the past. The request for one more goodnight kiss and one more "I love you, Daddy," never to be enjoyed or heard again.

My heart ached with a deeper pain than I had ever felt before. In my forty-one years of life on Earth, I thought I knew my fair share of pain, but absolutely nothing compared to the intensity of the pain I felt at that moment. The hole dove so deep and was so dark; I felt it might swallow me into its depths, where I would live forever.

If you are here, I know you can understand this pain—a pain so intense that it should be called something else, another name for deeper-than-deep pain. The agony is so extensive that you feel paralyzed. I am positive you understand this pain. I wish I could hug you right now and comfort you as the cascade of tears pour out. I would sit and listen and tell you I get it. Because I really do. Most of your friends and family will never fully understand the extent of your pain. Yes, they may have been through grief, but unless they have lost a spouse, they cannot relate to this earth-shattering pain.

As widows, our entire world has changed. We have a huge gaping hole in so many aspects of our lives, gaps our spouses used to fill. We shop differently, cook differently, watch TV differently, fall asleep differently, parent differently, do bills differently, fix things around the house differently, and so much more.

So, how in the world do we go on? How do we lift our heads off the pillow to face life without them? Those first days, there was absolute confusion and a blur of it all, like walking around in a nightmare. And when not sleeping, then curled up in the fetal position, struggling to breathe through the tears. But, you are going to make it! I made it past those first agonizing weeks, and you will too.

So, let's get started.

Your first goal is to get out of bed. It's okay to stay longer than you used to; I just don't want you to be stuck there for too long.

When we are in bed, we can't start living again. Just this one task seemed overwhelming to me. In my bed, I could bury myself under the covers and pretend my nightmare didn't exist. In the safety of my down comforter, I could cry and not face my forever-altered universe.

If we stay confined to our beds, we will never really live again. Picture your spouse right now. Remember their smile? They wouldn't want you to stay stuck in your sadness. They would want you to rise again. Maybe just that one thought will help you take the first step of lifting your head and putting your feet on the floor.

We have people around us who want to help. I want you to think of someone you can count on. Then, I want you to enlist this person to be your "wake-up friend" if you are not strong enough to get out of bed on your own right now. Ask them to call you or knock on your door every morning for as long as you need help. Do not be embarrassed to ask for this.

Another helpful thing was writing out something I was looking forward to the next day right before I went to bed. I still do this. Sometimes, I text it to myself so I will see it first thing in the morning. These little reminders help me to get up and face the day.

Additionally, when I take a few moments at the end of the day to reflect and write what I am thankful for, it helps me set my mind on the positive things. Philippians 4:8 (NIV) says:"*Finally, brothers and sisters, whatever is true, whatever is noble, whatever is right, whatever is pure, whatever is lovely, whatever is admirable—if anything is excellent or praiseworthy—think about such things.*" There are always positive things, even if they are hard to find.

Your mind is currently in the ICU. It needs special care and love right now. You need to make sure you are getting enough sleep. For the first few months, sleep was almost impossible for me. I missed my husband so much when the darkness fell, and the warmth of his body was absent. I have found several things that helped me sleep. I used prescription sleep aids for several months. After that, I used natural remedies like melatonin, and eventually, I could fall asleep on my own. Talk with your doctor if you feel you need something powerful—something prescription-strength.

Using apps that play soothing music and read Bible verses have been beneficial. It helps me focus my mind on God, and not the pain and darkness of the night.

I hope you feel equipped and ready to master Goal #1. It may take you a few days, or it may take you a few months. Whatever it is, it is okay. Every grief journey is unique. Yes, we share the same pain of losing our spouses, but our circumstances are different.

The most beautiful thing I have experienced is that, eventually, joy truly does come in the morning. The sun still rises, birds still chirp, and my heart still beats even through its brokenness. In this season of the deepest pain, I have felt God's most precious love. In my pain and sorrow, He meets me. He holds me and lets me cry until I have no more tears left inside.

Sometimes, I close my eyes and imagine climbing up on Jesus's lap like a small child. I lay my head on His chest and let the sobs come out. In a world where it feels like no human can fully relate to my pain, it feels so good to release it to God.

You, my friend, are not here by accident. You didn't pick this book up by chance; you were meant to be reading this at this exact moment in time. I am already praying for you, and since we know that prayer transcends all time, you are covered. What am I praying for? I am praying for you, my widow warrior sisters and brothers, that wherever you are in your widow journey, you will get to know Jesus for the first time or get to know Him more deeply.

You are not alone. I know there are times as a new widow that are excruciatingly painful and lonely. We can feel like we are alone, but we are not. As we draw close to the Heavenly Father, we can feel He has already drawn near to us. He has a special place in His heart for widows and will always make sure our needs are met. He also says He is close to the brokenhearted and saves those who are crushed in spirit (Psalm 34:18). That is us, my widow friends. We are crushed, and we are brokenhearted.

In *Widow Goals*, we will lock arms and press toward our goals together. Do you remember that childhood game called *Red Rover*? There was a line of people with locked arms. Someone would try to run through and break the bond of linked arms. We are the wall, with locked arms of love and understanding. Together, we will not be broken. The grief monster may try to break through, but with the strength of God, our love for each other, and the goals we have set before us, we cannot be broken.

Are you ready to continue this journey? My desire is for all of us to deeply heal. To move forward, we have to let ourselves feel today's pain with the hope of tomorrow. Let's do this thing!

Widow Reflections

1. What do you believe is keeping you here—on this earth—right now, in this season of deep pain? What if that reason is part of a bigger purpose you can't see yet?

2. When the weight of grief feels unbearable, what are the thoughts or truths that help you take just one more step? Is it faith? Love for your children? A promise you made? A whisper of hope?

3. If you could hear God say one thing to you this morning as you face the day, what would you want—or need—Him to say? Sit with that thought. Is it comfort? Is it purpose? Is it simply "I see you"?

Widow Action Steps

*Choose a small step to help you get out of bed tomorrow. Even if it feels like too much, set one small, doable intention for the morning.

*Reflect on how you've felt God's presence in your pain. Think back to a time you felt comforted, even in the middle of grief.

*Identify someone who can walk with you in this season.

Goal #2–Call on Your Tribe

"**C**ome to me, all you who are weary and burdened, and I will give you rest. Take my yoke upon you and learn from me, for I am gentle and humble in heart, and you will find rest for your souls. For my yoke is easy and my burden is light." Matthew 11:28–30 NIV

I'll never forget the first time I realized I couldn't do it all on my own. I was exhausted, numb, and just trying to make it through another day. The grief was crushing, the to-do list never-ending, and I still felt like I needed to hold it all together. But the truth is, I couldn't. And neither can you.

We were never meant to carry our burdens alone. We were created for connection—for community. And in the rawest moments of grief, when everything feels heavy and broken, one of the most powerful things you can do is call on your tribe.

A tribe is more than just a group of people—it's your lifeline. It's your go-to group that shows up in the middle of the night when you're falling apart. It's the friends who pray for you when you don't have the words, the family who brings a meal when you haven't eaten in days, the ones who cry with you without trying to fix it.

When my husband Luke was sick, I started leaning on my tribe in deeper ways. I created a group text with my closest friends and posted specific needs on Facebook. What I discovered is that most people want to help—they just don't know how. I learned that if I could be clear about what I needed, people were ready to step in.

After Luke died, my friends showed up in incredible ways. Within days, they brought meals, sat with me while I cried, created a fundraiser to help with burial costs, and just... stayed. I didn't have to entertain them or pretend to be okay. I could just be.

Every month, we had girls' nights where I could take off the mask and rest. I didn't have to be "mom" or "caretaker" or "widow"—I could just be Michelle. Sometimes we laughed until our sides hurt. Other times we cried through the entire evening. But I never felt alone.

My friends were such a huge help to me during this unbelievably hard time. But I had to be willing to accept the help—and so do you. Most people are well-meaning, but they don't know how to help us or what to do. This is when you must step up and let your tribe know what you need from them. Be as specific as you can. I wasn't shy about texting my tribe and letting them know what I needed to survive. Sometimes it was a quick "please pray for me," or "can anyone come over to help me with the house?"

I know we tend to believe we should be strong and do it all ourselves, but this is not the time to try to be Superwoman and handle everything on your own. Solitude is the best way to prolong your grieving. The idea that you need to grieve alone is one of the biggest myths about grief.

Jesus created us to live in community. I know sometimes you just want to run to your room, close the blinds, throw the covers over your head, and shut out the lights, the noise, and the people from the outside world. It is okay to visit this place, but you can't camp out there. Sometimes, a good sobbing cry does help. Please know that tears are healing; for what we feel, God can heal.

When Luke was sick (and he was sick for 16.5 of our 17 years of marriage), I tried daily to be Superwoman. I worked, cleaned, ran a business, drove my kids to all their activities, took care of Luke, attempted to cook, went running, wrote a book—and yes, I truly did it all. I tried so hard to be strong and appear strong to everyone, yet all the while, I was inwardly struggling to make it through another moment. There were times I was dying inside emotionally, and no one, not even Luke, knew it. The weight of his cancer diagnosis and additional sicknesses was almost too much for one person to handle. I wish I would have learned during those difficult years how to call on my tribe. I'll take an educated guess that if you are reading this, you can relate to what I'm describing.

I tried to be that woman for too many years.

Now that we recognize doing it all on our own is not the way to live life, we can learn to accept the help—and accept the gift of friends and family who want to support us. They want to come alongside us and lighten the load. Do you know who else wants to lighten your load? Jesus. He says His burden is light and His yoke is easy. As much as I love my friends and family—and while they do help me—their support is minimal in contrast to the rest and relief Jesus offers.

What does it mean that His yoke is easy? First, you have to understand what a yoke is. When Jesus talks about taking His yoke upon us, it's easy to picture something heavy, like the burdens we already carry. But a yoke isn't just a weight—it's a tool designed to share the load. In farming, a yoke connects two oxen so they can pull a heavy load together. The stronger ox helps guide and carry the weaker one, making the burden lighter than if either tried to pull it alone.

That's what Jesus is offering. He's saying, You don't have to do this by yourself. He's inviting us to be connected to Him, to let Him walk beside us, to match His steps to ours, and to take on the weight that feels too much for us to bear.

Grief, loneliness, and the overwhelming weight of trying to rebuild life after loss can feel crushing. But Jesus isn't adding another burden. His yoke is easy—not because life suddenly becomes simple, but because He is gentle and humble in heart. He carries what we can't.

This verse reminds us that we don't always have to be strong. We don't have to have it all figured out. We just have to say yes to His invitation. When we do, we find the rest we've been longing for—the kind that doesn't just ease our bodies but quiets our souls.

During my darkest moments—those times I cried face down on the bathroom floor, begging God to hear me, to heal me, to make me feel better—He always met me by covering me with peace and assuring me that I would get through this difficult journey. While everyone experiences the Holy Spirit differently, I feel an unexplainable peace come over my body, like I was floating. Although my world had just fallen apart when Luke breathed his last breath, and by the world's standards, I should have been anything but peaceful, the peace that passes all understanding permeated my weary body. He still continues to do this for me—and He wants to do it for you, too.

Take a moment to ask Jesus to cover you with the peace that passes all understanding. Ask Him to mend your broken heart. Invite Him into all the broken cracks in your soul. Jesus has a special place in His heart for widows, and He hears you, my friend. He actually knows and understands the pain you are going through, and He wants to make your burden light.

So, my friend, take a deep breath. You don't have to carry this alone. Call on your tribe, lean into the people who love you, and—most importantly—lean into Jesus. He's not standing at a distance waiting for you to figure it all out. He's right beside you, offering rest for your weary soul. Let Him carry what you were never meant to bear alone. When you surrender your pain, your exhaustion, and your overwhelming grief to Him, He replaces it with peace that doesn't even make sense—a peace that covers you in the middle of the storm.

You are not alone. You are deeply loved, held, and carried. All you have to do is say yes to His invitation.

Widow Reflections

1- Who is in your tribe? Make a list of the people you can lean on for support. If you're struggling to think of names, what steps can you take to start building a support system?

2- Have you been trying to carry your burdens alone? In what ways have you resisted asking for help—from others or from Jesus? How can you begin to surrender some of that weight?

3- What does "rest" look like for you? Jesus promises rest for our souls—how can you intentionally make space in your life to receive His peace and let Him carry your burdens?

Widow Action Steps

*Text or call one trusted person today and share how you're really doing.

*Write down three specific things you need help with this week—and ask someone to help.

*Spend five quiet minutes with Jesus, asking Him to lift your burden and fill you with His peace.

Goal #3–Let the Tears Flow Freely

"Y ou have kept count of my tossings; put my tears in your bottle. Are they not in your book?" Psalm 56:8 ESV

It happened in the middle of the grocery store aisle—tears fell without warning. All it took was a can of Chef Boyardee Beef Ravioli. The red label and smiling chef stared back at me, a painful reminder that I no longer needed to buy it. It was Luke's favorite, and just like that, the reality hit again: he was gone. I wasn't buying for him anymore. I wasn't buying for us. That one can opened a floodgate I couldn't stop. And I didn't try to. The can represented a grief so much deeper than I even understood at that moment; it was a void that I couldn't even fully comprehend.

Tears are our friends. The more we embrace the hurt and pain, the more quickly we will heal. I often describe grief like the old rhyme *We're Going on a Bear Hunt* [1] by Michael Rosen. When approaching an obstacle, the rhyme says:

> *Can't go under it,*
> *can't go over it,*
> *can't go around it,*
> *gotta go through it.*
> That is precisely like grief.

---

1. Rosen, Michael, and Helen Oxenbury. We're Going on a Bear Hunt. Margaret K. McElderry Books, 1989.

Unfortunately, there is no way around grief or the grieving process. We must push through the pain, agony, and ugliness evoked by grief to heal. In my work as a Grief Recovery Method Specialist, I have seen those who try to bury it. Consequently, they are still dealing with fresh grief years later because they never processed it, but instead, they buried it.

It is extremely important to feel our emotions; because I have experienced and firmly believe that what we feel, God can heal. Take a moment to let that sink in. The emotions we allow ourselves to feel are the ones that can truly be healed.

The reality is this: as a widow, there will be so many times when you feel the tears coming. DO NOT STUFF THEM DOWN. When you stifle those emotions, you only prolong the healing that God wants to do in your heart. The sooner you can let go of what people think about how you are grieving, the better. The reactions of others should be irrelevant because they are not experiencing your normal, grief-induced responses.

And yes, parents, I am talking to you as well. It is okay for our kids to see us cry and grieve. It gives them permission to feel what they are feeling and not suppress their emotions. However, there is a difference between allowing our kids to see us cry and you being stuck in bed, unable to care for them. We need to be able to tell the difference and avoid becoming stuck in a place where we cannot function for our kids. You know the ages and maturity of your children and can gauge what is appropriate for them.

There is also a difference between letting the tears flow freely and being perpetually stuck in your pain and sorrow. God's desire for you is to be whole and healed. He didn't allow you to go through this just to remain stuck in pain and sorrow for the rest of your life. If you're reading this, then God has a plan for you. As much as your heart breaks right now, and you feel like giving up, please don't. There will be a purpose for your pain. One day, it won't hurt so bad. One day, your mourning truly will be turned to dancing.

I can say this with passion and conviction because God did it for me.

In those first days of my pain, I thought I would never live to see joy again. My life felt like I was just existing. I felt like I had nothing to look forward to, and the pain was so intense that all I wanted to do was go back to bed and escape the reality of the pain so deep and dark that I could hardly breathe. Here is what I shared on social media on my 1st day of being a widow.

May 24th, 2020

Yesterday, I survived my first full day as a widow. So surreal. I woke up crying and felt like it was all a bad dream. I laid in bed for hours with Hayley as we cried and talked, and we were comforted by my sisters-in-law and best friend, Deborah. I finally got the strength to get out of bed and face the day. The first day without my Luke.

I talked with my counselor, hospice nurse, and so many people as we were surrounded by love. About a thousand times, I cried as I saw Luke's things where he had left them, like his prosthetic leg, hat, glasses, and clothes. I lost it when I saw our Christmas tree stand, as the thought of doing Christmas without Luke, who loved Christmas time to an extreme, was debilitating.

Everyone around me knew what to do without me even asking. Deborah took the kids out when I needed a moment to let out the agonizing pain I was feeling, and I laid in my mom's lap and cried and wailed from a place of pain I didn't even know was possible. My family came over and did all kinds of cleaning and projects that needed to get done; they didn't even ask; they just saw what needed to be done and did it. That is what I need right now: people who see a need and do it as I have no idea when asked what I really need. I have never felt the love and care of Jesus so much as I did while watching my house full of people working to help us.

We keep Luke's memory alive by constantly talking about him throughout the day and laughing with fun memories. But there is

*still an immense empty feeling in our house. Our hearts are break-
ing, and we are struggling with the last memories we have with Luke
as he didn't look like himself, and we are praying that we can just
remember him how he was with his most handsome smile. Please
pray for us in this area- I saw things the kids thankfully didn't that
were a bit traumatizing, and I want to get past that.
Hayley and I stayed up until after 2:00 AM talking, and I feel an even
deeper bond with her and all of the kids as we navigate through our
pain. There were moments yesterday when I thought I couldn't go
on, but then God gave me more strength. I know we will rise again,
and I KNOW God WILL make beauty out of these painful ashes, and
we will one day be able to make it through the day without crying.*

Those words convey the raw anguish of what I was going
through. The heartache was so deep and painful. That's where I
was the day after my husband died. But this is not an accurate rep-
resentation of where I am today, almost five years later, or where
I was even six months later. Part of my healing came because I
welcomed my tears any time, any place. I did not feel like I had to
explain or justify myself to anyone, and I also learned early in my
grief journey that tears were essential to my healing.

Isn't it amazing that God actually collects our tears in a bottle?
I picture that He either has a gigantic bottle for my tears or many
bottles! I love that even as vast as God is, He still takes the time to
collect our tears, every single one of them. That still is a concept
so grand I can scarcely comprehend it!

Grieving alongside your children is one of the most delicate
parts of widowhood. In the early days, I wrestled with whether to
cry in front of my kids. I didn't want to scare them or make them
feel like they had to take care of me. But over time, I learned the
importance of being real with them—within reason and depending
on their age.

For older children and teens, I found it helpful to let them see my tears. I wanted them to know that it's okay to feel and to express those feelings. I also learned, through experience and the wisdom of others, that sometimes it's best not to rush to comfort them in the middle of their crying. It can feel counterintuitive as a parent, but when we interrupt their tears too quickly, we may also be interrupting their grief process. Instead, I learned to sit with them, hold space, and let them cry—offering comfort and conversation afterward. My teens have come to understand that I do this not because I'm withholding comfort, but because I want them to fully feel and process their pain so they can move through it.

But this approach is different with younger children. If your child is very young, perhaps five or six, your presence and physical comfort while they're crying is essential. You are their anchor. After losing their parent, they may associate crying with something scary—like death. One mom shared that her daughter feared she was going to die next because she saw her crying. For that season, she chose to cry privately until her daughter could understand that grief doesn't equal danger. Then, she was able to model healthy sadness and explain her tears with reassurance. For littles, hugs, touch, and holding them during their tears are often the most healing response.

Ultimately, it comes down to knowing your child and their stage of development. What comforts one child might overwhelm another. And what's appropriate at one age may change as they grow. Our job is not to grieve perfectly—but to grieve with intentionality, honesty, and sensitivity, showing them that emotions are okay, and healing is possible.

My counselor once explained grief to my son in teenage-boy terms: When you don't deal with emotional pain, it's like constipation. You keep it in, and eventually, it explodes—and it's not pretty. It might be a bit graphic, but it drives the point home: holding it in only creates more damage. Let the tears come.

So, friend, let the tears flow. Don't resist them. Don't apologize for them. Let them wash over you and release what your heart can't carry alone. Your tears are not a sign of weakness—they are a sign of love, of letting go, and of healing. Each one is precious to God and part of your journey toward peace. Don't be afraid of your tears. They are leading you somewhere new. Let them fall, and let Him heal.

Widow Reflections

1. Reflect on a time when you felt the need to hold back your tears in grief. What stopped you from letting them flow freely? How might embracing those emotions have brought you closer to healing?

2. How do you handle grief around others—especially your children or close family? What might it look like to create a safe space where you and your loved ones can grieve openly and honestly?

3. Psalm 56:8 says that God collects our tears in His bottle. What does this imagery mean to you personally? How does it affect the way you see your grief?

Widow Action Steps

*Give yourself permission to cry—wherever and whenever the tears come. Whether it's in the car, at the store, or late at night, don't hold them back. Let your body and heart release the pain.

*Tell a trusted friend or family member how you're really feeling. Don't pretend you're okay if you're not. Say the hard things out loud. Sharing your pain is a brave step toward healing.

*Write a journal entry or prayer pouring out your emotions. Let it be raw, honest, and unfiltered. God isn't afraid of your pain—and neither should you be.

Goal #4–Remember to Take Care of Yourself

"**D**o you not know that your bodies are temples of the Holy Spirit, who is in you, whom you have received from God? You are not your own." — 1 Corinthians 6:19 NIV

In the whirlwind of grief, it's easy to forget that your body and soul are still here—still worthy of care, still carrying you through each painful step. You might feel like a shell of yourself, just barely surviving. But I want to gently remind you of something important: taking care of yourself is not selfish—it's essential.

I know this concept can seem easy in theory but incredibly challenging to implement in reality. When we lose our spouse, our entire sense of time, space, and purpose feels off. If we have children at home, their needs often take priority, and in taking care of them, we can forget to take care of ourselves.

But the truth remains: you have to put on your own oxygen mask before you can help anyone else. I know you've probably heard that a hundred times, but I'm saying it again—because it's that important.

So, how do you actually put this into practice when you feel like you're barely functioning?

You enlist your tribe (see Chapter 2).

For me, during those first few weeks and months, my mom helped me survive. She showed up. She took care of the kids, made sure we ate, and simply let me cry. I remember one moment vividly—just days after Luke died—I crawled into her lap as a 41-year-old woman and cried from a place so broken, so deep, I didn't know healing was even possible. And she held me. And through her care, she helped me begin the process of taking care of myself when I couldn't do it alone. She reminded me that the dark tunnel wouldn't last forever, and her love helped me find even the faintest light at the end of it.

Eventually, I got to a place where I could do more for myself. I know your world might feel like it's spinning uncontrollably right now, and there are so many things that demand your attention. —But if you don't put your oxygen mask on quickly, you won't be able to help anyone else, no matter how much you want to.

So what does taking care of yourself actually look like?

Let's start with something simple that is so easily forgotten in the early times of grief—remembering to eat. Even if you have no appetite, do it anyway. Your body needs fuel, and not just any fuel. Choose what is nutritious for you. This means real, whole foods—fruits, vegetables, and things that nourish your body, instead of depleting it. You are probably already exhausted; the last thing your body needs is to fight through processed food on top of your physical and emotional fatigue.

Accountability became a vital part of my healing journey. Every time I met with my counselor, she asked the same simple but powerful question: "What are you doing for you?" Over time, that question began to shift my perspective. I started anticipating it and intentionally looked for ways to care for myself—because I knew she would ask. Sometimes the answer was small: a bubble bath, a quiet walk, or lunch with a friend. But it was never really about the activity itself—it was about the intention behind it.

These were moments where no one needed me, and I could simply exist. They were soul-filling pauses in the middle of the chaos. One of the most impactful outlets for me became the gym. It gave me strength, clarity, and space—physically and mentally—to breathe, to release, and to rebuild. If your spouse passed after a long illness, there's a good chance you've been putting yourself last for a long time. It's time to turn that around. In order to be the best mom, friend, sister, daughter, or whatever roles you carry—you have to make yourself a priority again.

Not someday.

Now.

One of the ways I created space to care for myself was by developing a simple morning routine. I first heard the concept on [1] *The Mel Robbins Podcast*, in an episode called "Try it for 1 Day: Do this Every Morning to Boost Motivation & Focus." I had read plenty of books about morning routines, but they always felt overwhelming or unrealistic, especially ones that required waking up at 5:00 a.m. I knew that wouldn't work for me. But Mel's version was simple, doable, and could be done anywhere. That's what made it stick.

Now, the first thing I do when I wake up is get out of bed right away. Let's be honest—yes, I go to the bathroom first (don't we all?). Then I make my bed. This was never a habit for me before, but now it gives me a small sense of accomplishment and helps keep me from climbing back under the covers. I head straight for a glass of water—before any caffeine. Mel Robbins encourages waiting at least an hour after waking before having caffeine. Although this was initially difficult, I got used to it, and I really do feel the difference.

---

1. Mel Robbins, "Try It For 1 Day: Do This Every Morning to Boost Motivation & Focus," The Mel Robbins Podcast, January 13, 2025,

Next, I go outside to walk for 10 minutes in the sunlight. If it's raining, I use the treadmill. And here's the key—I leave my phone inside. I don't even look at it until all of this is done. Once you pick up that phone, you're in reaction mode, responding to everyone else's needs. This time is sacred, so I protect it fiercely.

When I come back inside, I spend some time reading and praying. This interval of quiet grounds me and connects me spiritually before the chaos of the day begins. And then I do a thing that might make you roll your eyes—I give myself a high five in the mirror. I touch the glass, look myself in the eye, and smile. At first, it felt awkward and even silly. I've definitely had to explain it a few times when someone walked in mid-high-five. But here's the thing—it works.

Science shows that giving yourself a high five triggers positive neural responses in your brain. According to Mel Robbins, who popularized this idea, the act of a high five releases dopamine and activates the same parts of your brain that light up when you receive encouragement from others. Over time, this simple gesture can help rewire your self-talk, boost your mood, and set a more empowered tone for the day. So go ahead—try it. You might be surprised how powerful such a small act can be.

These habits now anchor me. I often add in journaling or make a list of things I want to accomplish. This whole routine helps me feel centered—physically, emotionally, and spiritually—before I turn my attention to everyone else. And if you have small children or other circumstances that make mornings impossible, find another time that works. Just find the time. Even if it's only ten or fifteen minutes, that time matters. Guard it like your life depends on it—because in some ways, it does.

Taking care of yourself is not optional—it's foundational. It's not a luxury; it's a necessity. And it's not selfish—it's sacred.

I know this journey is hard. There are days when just getting out of bed feels like a victory. But little by little, as you take small steps towards caring for yourself again, you'll find strength returning. You'll start to feel a little more like *yourself*. And from that place of healing, you'll be better equipped to love and lead those around you.

You matter. Your body matters. Your soul matters.

Take care of it, it's been through a lot.

Widow Reflections

1. When was the last time you did something just for yourself—and how did it make you feel?

2. What beliefs might be holding you back from prioritizing your own well-being right now?

3. How can you reframe self-care as a form of strength instead of weakness?

Widow Action Steps

*Create a simple morning routine, start with one or two small things: making your bed, stepping outside, drinking a glass of water, or reading a short devotional.

*Plan one self-care activity this week Pick something that feeds your soul—whether it's a walk, a nap, lunch with a friend, or a workout. Put it on your calendar like it matters. Because it does.

*Choose one nourishing food to prioritize daily Even if you're not hungry, commit to fueling your body. Think of one healthy, go-to snack or meal you can keep on hand and aim to eat it at least once each day.

Goal #5- Don't Be Surprised by Anxiety

"Do not be anxious about anything, but in everything by prayer and supplication with thanksgiving let your requests be made known to God. And the peace of God, which surpasses all understanding, will guard your hearts and your minds in Christ Jesus." Philippians 4:6-7 ESV

The pain in my left calf was sudden and sharp. "This has to be a blood clot," I panicked silently. It was only three days after Luke died, and since a blood clot was what ultimately took his life, my mind instantly went there. My heart raced. I woke up my daughter Hayley, who was sleeping beside me. "Hayley, help me!" I said frantically. I stood, and everything went black. I collapsed. In the background, I could hear Hayley praying.

Eventually, I made it back to bed, shaken but unharmed. That moment marked the beginning of something I had never experienced before: anxiety.

In my younger years, I was carefree and full of life. I'd hop in the car with my best friends, windows down, bathing suits on under our clothes, chasing sun-soaked lunches in the park and dreaming about our futures. I lived fully and fearlessly.

Then cancer walked in and dimmed the light. Luke was sick for 16 and a half of our 17 married years. But even during that time, I wasn't an anxious person. Anxiety didn't grip me until after Luke died.

A few weeks after the "blood clot scare," I was sanitizing my countertops with a Lysol wipe, and for some strange reason, I smelled the wipe and instantly went into full-blown panic mode. The room began to go dim, and I once again began to feel faint. My mind irrationally thought I had done permanent damage.

After a few more episodes, I visited a doctor who explained how powerful the brain is—how the pain I felt was real, even though the cause wasn't. She helped me see how my mind had learned fear, and now it was on autopilot.

It all made sense to me when I read the book called *Anxiety: The Missing Stage of Grief* by Claire Bidwell Smith[1]. Although I know there are no stages of grief (we will cover this in another chapter), I learned through these pages that anxiety is natural after the death of a loved one, especially if you watched your loved one die. Claire says,

"After the death of a loved one, many of the fears that run through your mind can be perceived as more of a threat than before the loss. You have witnessed someone die now that inevitability is more real than ever before in your life. So when you have a fear-based thought about your own mortality, or a worry about losing someone else, your body and mind are reacting stranger than before you experienced loss."

And so, my battle began. But here's the good news: there are parts of anxiety we can take back.

Now, please hear me out. I am not a medical doctor, and I am not trying to make any medical claims. We are each on an individual journey. If you need help managing your anxiety, please seek professional support. However, I am speaking from my own experience and explaining methods I found successful.

---

1. Claire Bidwell Smith, Anxiety: The Missing Stage of Grief (New York: Da Capo Lifelong Books, 2018). Used with permission

For me, anxiety was often tied to my health. I feared leaving my children alone. Every ache, every strange sensation, felt like a death sentence. I still have moments, but now I know how to fight back.

2 Corinthians 10:5 (ESV) says: *"We destroy arguments and every lofty opinion raised against the knowledge of God, and take every thought captive to obey Christ."*

What does it mean to take a thought captive? It means you don't just let it pass—you stop it. You confront it. You ask it: *"Where did you come from?"* and *"Who sent you?"* And then you replace it with truth.

In one of my darkest moments, I heard, "Where is God now?" But I fought back:

"God is for me and not against me. He works ALL things together for good. He will never leave me or forsake me." (Romans 8:31, Romans 8:28, Hebrews 13:5)

Years ago, a counselor taught me about Automatic Negative Thoughts (ANT's). These are those sneaky lies your brain throws at you. They start as small snowballs. One negative thought finds another and another—until the small snowballs turns into an avalanche.

But you can interrupt that spiral with "ANT eaters"—truth statements that shut down the lies.

Example: The thought "No one cares about me anymore" can trigger a memory of the friend who hasn't called... and another... and suddenly, you're drowning. Your ANT eater might be:

"I have many people who care for me. Life gets busy, but I am loved and not forgotten."

Nobody told me that anxiety might hit after loss. I want *you* to know: it's normal. It doesn't mean you're weak. It means you're human, and your world just changed forever.

When God says, "Be *anxious for nothing*," He also promises peace. A peace that *guards*—actively protects—our hearts and minds.

What if, instead of spiraling, we *first* prayed? What if we truly believed Luke 12:25: "*And which of you by being anxious can add a single hour to his span of life?*"

Anxiety after loss is not a failure of faith—it's a response of a heart that has been through trauma. But God does not leave us there.

Philippians 4:6-7 isn't just a command to "be anxious for nothing"—it's an invitation to trade our panic for peace. How? Through prayer. Through surrender. Through bringing every fear, every ache, and every unknown to God. When we do, something supernatural happens: His peace shows up. Not the kind that makes sense, but the kind that carries us anyway. A peace that guards—puts a shield around—both our hearts and our minds.

I won't pretend this is easy. I still have to take anxious thoughts captive almost daily. But over time, I've learned that fear doesn't get the final word. God does.

So if you're waking up with your heart pounding, or staring at the ceiling wondering what's next, know this: you're not broken. You're grieving. And God is near to the brokenhearted.

Breathe. Pray. Speak truth. And remember—you are not alone, and anxiety doesn't get to write your story. God does.

Widow Reflections

1. Philippians 4:6-7 encourages prayer and thanksgiving to combat anxiety. When has prayer brought peace in your life?

2. What are some ANT's that creep in during your grief? What "ANT eater" truths can you speak over them?

3. Understanding anxiety as part of grief can help normalize it. What small strategy from this chapter can you try this week?

Widow Action Steps

*Identify a trusted friend or family member you can call during moments of anxiety.

*Write our your ANT eaters and keep them where you can see them.

*Commit to praying when anxiety rises and invite God to guard your heart with peace.

Goal #6–Reenter Social Spaces with Confidence

"**S**o do not throw away your confidence; it will be richly rewarded." Hebrews 10:35 NIV

I remember walking into my first big social event about a month after Luke died. It was a huge Fourth of July party. I felt the gaze of acquaintances who didn't know what to say. People seemed to disappear so they didn't have to talk to me. But one kind and compassionate woman — barely more than an acquaintance — looked me in the eyes and simply said, "I am so sorry about Luke."

That was all I needed: someone, anyone, to acknowledge that my life had stopped. Someone willing to sacrifice their own comfort to enter into my pain. I didn't fall apart or cry hysterically; I simply said thank you and walked away feeling seen.

Do you know that feeling when the world just keeps going, even though your entire universe has stopped? That's how I felt every day during those first few months. I'll never forget going grocery shopping just a few days after Luke died. It was surreal — almost like an out-of-body experience.

So many thoughts ran through my head:

- Do they know my husband just died?

- Why are they so happy?

- How are they okay when I'm barely functioning?

Meanwhile, I was struggling to keep my cart in a straight line, surrounded by people happily choosing apples and bananas — as if nothing had changed. But everything had changed for me.

So, how do we make it bearable to be in social situations again? How do we move from the comfort of our sweatpants to the seemingly unbearable outside world?

Here's the truth: whether it's out of necessity or desire, at some point you will have to reenter society. Life won't always feel this overwhelming. The transition doesn't happen overnight — it happens slowly, one day, one moment, one experience at a time.

Yes, we absolutely need time alone to grieve and process. But we also need community. In the beginning, you may have to force yourself to leave the house. For me, even getting dressed felt like a monumental task. That's okay.

Let me break it down into simple, manageable steps.

Start small. Your first outing doesn't have to be a crowded party. Ask a trusted friend to meet you for coffee, lunch, or a walk. Let them know you'll need them to plan the details — and that showing up will take everything you've got.

Decide in advance that you will go, even if you don't feel like it when the time comes. You know it's good for your emotional health, and those first few moments of discomfort are often the hardest.

During the outing, be yourself. Cry if you feel like crying. Laugh if you feel like laughing. You don't have to perform — just show up as you are.

When you get home, reflect on how it felt. You might be exhausted, but there's a high chance it felt good to get out of the house. It might even feel like a small victory.

When you feel ready, try your first big outing. Like my Fourth of July party, it may feel awkward, disorienting, or emotionally overwhelming. That's okay.

People may not know how to act around you. Some will avoid you. Others might say the wrong thing. Try to give them grace and listen for their heart, not just their words (we'll cover more on this in another chapter).

Another gentle reentry strategy: visit a farmer's market, craft fair, or similar event. These places let you be around people without the pressure to engage. You can quietly walk, observe, or leave without anyone noticing.

Pro tip: Always have an exit strategy. Drive yourself if possible, so you can leave when needed. That way, you can give yourself permission to step away without guilt or awkwardness.

Once you've dipped your toes into a few social outings, consider volunteering. It's an incredible way to shift your focus, serve others, and begin to rediscover purpose.

When I volunteer, I take my eyes off my own pain and pour into others. It doesn't mean my grief disappears, but I've found so much healing in helping others heal. If you attend a church, they likely have plenty of volunteer opportunities. If not, a quick social media post or Google search can help you find something meaningful in your area.

Take note of how you feel after each experience. Journaling is a safe and healing way to process your emotions. I wrote every day in my early widowhood, and looking back on those entries reminds me of how far God has brought me.

I've kept journals since I was nine years old — one of my earliest was a prayer journal from third grade. Writing helps us reflect, release, and see the thread of God's presence even when we feel lost.

Every small outing is a step toward reclaiming your life. Don't underestimate the power of getting dressed, putting on makeup, and choosing something that makes you feel good about yourself. It's not shallow — it's self-care. It's confidence-building. And it matters.

If you're reading this, it's because God still has purpose for your life. Even if it doesn't feel that way right now, I promise — He does. He turns mourning into dancing. He brings beauty from ashes.

You are not the same person you were before your loss—and you're not meant to be. Grief has changed you, yes, but it has also refined you. With each courageous step into the world, you are declaring that your story isn't over. You are living proof that broken hearts can still beat with purpose. As you reenter social spaces, remember this: you carry the light of someone you loved and lost, and God is not finished with you yet. You were created for connection, for purpose, for impact. So lift your head, step out in faith, and walk boldly into the life still waiting for you.

Widow Reflections

1. What emotions rise up when you think about being around people again?

2. Who in your life feels safe, comforting, or supportive — and how might they help you take a small step back into community?

3. How have you seen God's presence with you during moments of loneliness or discomfort?

Widow Action Steps

*Ask a trusted friend to meet for coffee, go for a walk, or visit a farmers market. Let them know you may need help with logistics — and that just showing up is a big win.

*Choose something that makes you feel confident. Take time to get ready as an act of self-care. Pray, journal, or listen to worship music to calm any anxiety before leaving.

*Jot down what went well and how you felt emotionally. What helped? What was hard? Use this reflection to plan your next step — remember, this is a process, not a race.

Goal #7–Focus on Today

"**T**herefore do not worry about tomorrow, for tomorrow will worry about itself. Each day has enough trouble of its own."
— *Matthew 6:34, NIV*

When you think about the future, does it feel like a giant tidal wave threatening to pull you under? Does your mind spin in a thousand directions, leaving you paralyzed and overwhelmed? Maybe the thought of the next month—or even the next week—makes you want to pull the covers over your head and escape the reality of today.

If so, you're not alone. When we lose our spouse, our brains go into what I like to call the ICU. And not just figuratively—it's as if our minds and hearts have been admitted to an actual Intensive Care Unit. Life doesn't function the way it used to, and honestly, we can't expect it to.

Grief has a way of flipping everything upside down. Tasks that once seemed small or automatic now feel insurmountable. I used to be the glue in my friend group—the one organizing girls' nights, setting dates, and making sure everyone showed up. It brought me joy to connect people and create space for community. But after my husband died, I couldn't handle that role anymore. Even selecting a date on the calendar felt like climbing a mountain.

Eventually, I reached out to my friends and said, "I need you to be the glue for now." And they stepped up. They planned, and I simply showed up. Over time, as I healed, I regained the desire and ability to be that connector again. But it took time, grace, and help to get there.

In those early days, even focusing on just one day felt like too much. I remember mornings when simply getting out of bed felt overwhelming. My to-do list seemed a mile long—take care of the kids, feed the dog, pay the bills, run errands. It all felt impossible.

So I broke it down further. If a day was too much, I focused on the next hour. And if that was still too much, I focused on the next minute.

Sometimes surviving grief isn't about big victories—it's about small ones: getting dressed, eating a meal, or making it through the next 10 minutes. And while those things might not sound like much, each one is a victory. Every time you move forward, even just a little, you are proving to yourself that you are resilient and capable.

When you're grieving, your mind is constantly fighting two battles: one against the weight of the past and one against the uncertainty of the future. The past holds the memories of what you've lost, and the future seems like a dark, uncharted territory. It's easy to feel stuck in the middle.

But here's the truth: the only place you can truly live is the present. God gives us strength for today—not for yesterday, not for tomorrow, but for *this* moment. When you try to carry the weight of the past and the future all at once, it's no wonder you feel like collapsing. Focusing on today doesn't mean forgetting the past or ignoring the future. It means trusting that God will carry you—one day at a time.

So how do you stay rooted in the present?

Here are a few things that helped me:

1. Set Micro-Goals

On days when everything felt overwhelming, I gave myself one simple task: make the bed. That's it. Once that was done, I gave myself permission to rest or move on to the next small thing. One tiny step at a time. Eventually, those micro-goals helped me feel a bit more in control. Even on the hardest days, I could say, "I accomplished something today." And that mattered.

2. Create a Routine

Grief throws your entire life into chaos, so routines can be a lifesaver. For me, that looked like starting each day with prayer and writing down one thing I was thankful for. Even if it was just "The sun is shining today" it reminded me there was still good in the world.

3. Ask for Help

There's no shame in it. Maybe you need someone to handle groceries or simply be with you. Or maybe, like me, you just need to tell a friend, "I can't be the glue right now." People want to help. You just have to let them.

4. Lean on Scripture

Matthew 6:34 became my lifeline:

"Therefore do not worry about tomorrow, for tomorrow will worry about itself." (NIV)

Another verse that strengthened me was:

"So do not fear, for I am with you; do not be dismayed, for I am your God. I will strengthen you and help you." Isaiah 41:10, NIV

God didn't ask me to figure everything out. He asked me to trust Him—for today.

5. Give Yourself Permission to Rest

Some days, doing nothing is the most healing thing you can do. Rest isn't laziness—it's recovery. You are not failing when you rest; you're honoring what your body and soul need.

In the beginning, there were people around—meals delivered, calls coming in. But as time passed, the world kept spinning while mine felt stuck. That's when focusing on just one day became my lifeline. Maybe today you write in a journal, cry with a friend, or pull out a photo and remember. Or maybe you just whisper, "God, I need You right now."

I used to go on walks and talk out loud to God—pouring out my fear, my questions, and my heartbreak. It didn't fix everything, but it reminded me I wasn't alone.

And friend, neither are you.

The heaviness won't last forever. One day, you'll laugh again. You'll plan again. You'll even hope again. But for now, just focus on today. Or the next hour. Or even just the next breath. God will meet you there.

Each small victory is proof that you're moving forward, even when it doesn't feel like it. You're doing the best you can—and that's enough.

Widow Reflections

1. When have you felt overwhelmed by thoughts of the future, and what small step helped bring you back to the present?

2. What's one small victory you've had this week that deserves to be acknowledged and celebrated?

3. What does "trusting God for today" look like for you right now?

Widow Action Steps

*Choose one micro-goal to accomplish today. Start small: make the bed, go for a walk, eat a meal, or drink water. Celebrate the small win.

*Create or adjust a simple daily routine. Pick one thing to do every day—prayer, journaling, stretching, or listing one thing you're grateful for.

*Reach out for help or encouragement. Text a trusted friend, join a support group, or ask someone to pray for you. Let someone into your journey.

Goal #8–Let Go of Why

"Trust in the Lord with all your heart and lean not on your own understanding; in all your ways submit to Him, and He will make your paths straight." Proverbs 3:5–6 NIV

Why did our spouses die? Why are we alone? Why are our children fatherless?

I wish I had the answer to these and so many more unanswered questions. When Luke died, I told my children that we won't understand until we get to heaven. I explained that our lives are like a puzzle—we can only see individual pieces, but God sees the whole picture and understands why things happen. It's a simple explanation, but difficult to truly grasp.

There are so many questions we'll never know the answers to this side of heaven. I used to ask, "Why me? Why my husband?" The unknowns were overwhelming until I came to a life-changing realization: *If God allowed it, I can accept it.*

I remember hearing a sermon that helped me make sense of the chaos. The pastor said that everything must pass through God's hands—He either causes it or allows it. We know that God does not cause sickness and death, but if it happened, then He allowed it. That one sentence—"If God allowed it, I can accept it"—is small in size but huge in meaning. It has the power to shift your entire perspective.

When we stay stuck in the "why me?" cycle, we can't move forward. Our eyes get fixed on ourselves and our painful circumstances. True healing becomes nearly impossible when we're consumed by the same unanswerable question over and over. I believe this is one of the enemy's greatest tactics—to keep us in a pit of despair. When we're consumed by our own pain, we can't be used by God to help others.

I remember one of the hardest days early on. It was my first Thanksgiving without Luke. To change things up, I took my kids to Great Wolf Lodge. I sat in a chair by the water park, watching them play, while family after family walked by—each one with a mom and a dad. Tears streamed down my face as sad music played through my AirPods. My heart screamed, *This isn't fair. Why me? Why my kids?*

I was texting with a friend, pouring out my pain. She gently encouraged me to turn off the sad music and focus on the good in front of me—my kids, their laughter, the fact that we were together. I took her advice. As soon as I stopped feeling sorry for myself and brought my attention back to the present moment, everything started to feel just a little bit lighter.

That moment taught me something I want to pass on to you: when you catch yourself spiraling into a "why me?" moment, stop and say out loud at least three things you're thankful for. Go ahead—do it now. Wherever you are, speak them out. Don't worry about what the person next to you might think. This is for your heart, your health, and your healing. It may feel awkward at first, but gratitude is powerful—it shifts our focus from what we've lost to what we still have.

Jesus never promised us a trouble-free life. In fact, He told us plainly that trouble was inevitable:

"I have told you these things, so that in me you may have peace. In this world you will have trouble. But take heart! I have overcome the world." John 16:33 NIV

He didn't promise to remove the fire in our lives, but He promised to be with us in it. He didn't say we wouldn't walk through deep waters, but He said we wouldn't drown.

I remember many times throughout Luke's cancer journey when I felt like I was drowning. The weight of caring for three kids, a very sick husband, and managing our financial situation was crushing. During one of Luke's hospital stays, his doctor told me he had a 50% chance of survival.

I didn't cry in front of him—I couldn't. I held it together until I could sneak away to the hospital chapel. I walked in, closed the door, and sat down, tears threatening to break free. I remembered a picture a friend had once sent me—Jesus reaching down into the water to rescue someone. I closed my eyes and imagined myself underwater, and Jesus grabbing my hand and lifting me up.

That moment didn't erase the pain, but it gave me a visual reminder that I wasn't alone. Even when I felt completely submerged by fear and grief, I was being carried by the One who would not let me sink. That image became a turning point for me. It helped me begin the process of letting go of the "why?"

The "why" can be suffocating. It locks us in a state of endless questioning and self-pity. It keeps us focused on the unfairness of our situation rather than the grace that could carry us through it. The truth is, asking "why?" repeatedly doesn't change what happened. It doesn't bring back our loved ones. It doesn't ease the pain. And it doesn't help us heal.

Instead of asking "Why me?" or "Why my spouse?" we can begin to ask new, more productive questions:

- *What now? What can I learn from this? How can I use this pain to help others? What is God trying to teach me through this experience?*

These questions lead us forward. They create space for growth, transformation, and healing.

Letting go of "why" doesn't mean we ignore our pain or pretend everything is fine. It means accepting that we may never understand. And that's okay. We can still trust God's plan even when the picture isn't clear.

When I finally accepted that I might never know why Luke had to die, I began to shift my focus. I started looking for meaning in the middle of the mess. I found strength in knowing I wasn't the only one to walk through deep suffering. I discovered purpose in offering hope to others on a similar path.

It's not easy to let go of "why." As humans, we long for answers and explanations. But sometimes, there just aren't any. Sometimes, we have to trust that God has a reason for what He allows, even when it breaks our hearts.

"For my thoughts are not your thoughts, neither are your ways my ways," declares the Lord. "As the heavens are higher than the earth, so are my ways higher than your ways and my thoughts than your thoughts." Isaiah 55:8–9 NIV

These verses gently remind me that I don't have to understand everything. I just need to have faith—faith that God is still good, even in the most painful circumstances. His ways may not always make sense, but they are always rooted in love.

Please be kind to yourself on this journey. There's no shame in asking "why" or feeling frustrated by the lack of answers. But what matters most is how we respond to those questions. Will we stay stuck, or will we choose to move forward?

Letting go of "why" doesn't happen overnight. It's a daily process. Some days, the questions will sneak back in. That's okay. But as you keep trusting God, you'll find the need for answers slowly fading, replaced by peace.

Remember: healing doesn't mean forgetting your loved one or your pain. It means learning to live with it while believing God still has good things ahead for you.

You don't need all the answers to move forward. You just need to trust that God has them. And that's enough.

Widow Reflections

1. What "why" questions have you been carrying since your loss?

2. How have those questions helped—or hindered—your healing?

3. What would it look like to release your "why" to God today?

Widow Action Steps

*Say three things you're thankful for out loud whenever you begin to spiral into "why me."

*Write down your biggest "why" questions and then pray, offering each one to God.

*Create a "Peace Journal" where you record moments of comfort, reminders of God's presence, or clarity in your grief journey.

Goal #9–Discover Your New Normal

"**H**e has made everything beautiful in its time." Ecclesiastes 3:11 ESV

From the moment Luke died, I knew life as I had known it would never be the same. The silence in our home was almost physical—his glasses still on the nightstand, a half-full cup of water, the pain pills he never got to take. Sacred remnants of the life we once shared.

I remember walking back into our house for the first time after he was gone and collapsing onto the bedroom floor. His prosthetic leg leaned against the bed—haunting proof that he was really, truly gone. I didn't need to replay the events of that morning. They were already etched in my soul. It was the aftermath that undid me—the absence. The new reality I had to somehow live in.

Normal life? That concept felt completely foreign. Honestly, what even was normal? Nearly all of our 17 years of marriage had been spent in and out of hospitals. Luke was diagnosed with cancer just a few months after our wedding. Ambulance rides, chemo treatments, middle-of-the-night emergencies—they shaped our rhythm, our resilience, our routine.

And yet we had joy. Our children, all born within just three and a half years, filled our days with laughter and chaos. Luke was present for every milestone he could manage—sports games, plays, even just sitting beside them while they watched TV. He did his best, even through pain. Our life wasn't easy, but it was ours.

And then, one day, it wasn't. Luke died. Suddenly, I was alone.

A kind hospice nurse had once warned me that no matter how much I'd prepared, it would still feel like the ground had disappeared beneath me. She was right.

Our home now echoed with quiet. The kind of quiet that doesn't soothe—it isolates. And I asked myself: How could anything about this be normal again?

The answer? It wouldn't be. Not the old normal, anyway. But slowly, piece by piece, I began to discover a new one.

This is one of the hardest realities of grief—we must release what was, and learn to embrace what is. It doesn't happen all at once. In the beginning, all we do is long for the life we had. We replay the past and resist the present. But slowly, moment by moment, we begin to step into a new way of being. It's unfamiliar. It's uncomfortable. But it is where healing begins.

And here's the good news: this new normal, though different, can still be beautiful.

As time passed, I began to see glimpses of light. It didn't come in grand, sweeping moments—but in tiny flickers. Laughter with my children. A sunrise that reminded me I was still alive. The kindness of a friend. God began to piece my heart back together, not to restore what was, but to create something new—something sacred.

Let me share a visual that helped me understand this process. It's an activity I did at a widow's retreat, and I invite you to try it too.

1. Find a breakable item — a clay pot, plate, or mug. Paint or draw a picture on it that represents your life before your spouse died. You don't need artistic skill—just honesty. Include anything that symbolized your "before."

2. Admire your creation. Look at it. Reflect on what it represents—your life before the loss. Remember the love, the laughter, and even the struggles.

3. Break it. Yes—break it. Throw it or drop it on concrete. Let this represent the moment your life shattered. It's okay to cry. Let yourself feel it.

4. Sit with the broken pieces. Notice how some don't fit back together. Some may be missing. That's what grief feels like—like trying to rebuild a life that no longer fits the same way.

5. Imagine Jesus with you. Picture Him kneeling beside you, gently taking your hand, offering new pieces—sea glass blue, radiant purple, soft greens, pinks. He looks in your eyes and says, "Your life will never look the same, but I am giving you something new. I am making something beautiful. Do you trust Me?"

6. Create something new. Using a different base—like a wooden coaster or small canvas—glue the broken pieces and new colored ones into a mosaic. We used wooden coasters at the retreat. Let this represent your new normal—still broken, still real, but also vibrant and beautiful in a new way.

Tears may stream down your cheeks as Jesus gathers your brokenness. This is the moment of choice. Will you accept these new pieces? Will you trust that beauty can be born from devastation?

It's tempting to cling to the past—to try to recreate it, to live inside of memories. But friend, I am living proof that letting Jesus craft something new will lead to beauty you never imagined. It doesn't mean the journey is easy. It doesn't mean you'll stop missing your spouse. But it does mean you'll start living again.

You don't have to let go of the memories—those are treasures. But you do have to let go of the expectation that your life will ever look the same. That's scary, I know. We like the familiar. But truly—what other choice do we have?

You can either live in the painful past, or you can choose to trust the One who knows how to turn ashes into beauty. Your life may never look like it once did—but that doesn't mean it won't be beautiful again. God isn't asking you to forget the past. He's asking you to place it in His hands so He can begin something new.

You are not just surviving.
You are becoming.
And what you're becoming is
sacred,
whole,
and beautifully made.

Widow Reflections

1. What parts of your "old normal" are you still trying to hold on to?

2. What small moments of peace, joy, or light have you noticed in your new normal—and how did they make you feel?

3. How might it feel to let Jesus give you new pieces for the life ahead?

Widow Action Steps

*Try the Broken Pot Activity- Paint, break, and add the mosaic pieces and reflect. Let it represent the moment your life changed and invite Jesus into the pieces.

*Name One New Beauty-Write down one beautiful thing that has come from this hard journey—however small.

*Speak a Declaration-Say aloud: "Jesus, I trust You to create something beautiful from my broken pieces." Repeat this daily and journal how your heart responds.

Goal #10 – Let Yourself Laugh

"**S**he is clothed with strength and dignity; she can laugh at the days to come." Proverbs 31:25 NIV

Laugh. I'm serious.

Try to make yourself laugh right now. I know it might feel forced, awkward, or even impossible—but just try it. Why? Because laughter is one of grief's greatest gifts. And the moment you allow yourself to smile again, something inside you begins to heal.

Have you allowed yourself to truly laugh since your spouse died? Maybe you have—and then felt that wave of guilt crash over you right afterward.

I remember exactly how it felt the first time I really laughed after Luke died. It wasn't a quiet giggle. It was a full-on, from-the-belly, can't-breathe kind of laugh. And almost instantly, the guilt flooded in. How can I laugh when Luke just died? Is this okay? Am I moving on too fast? Wasn't I supposed to be sad every minute of every day?

But friend—those thoughts couldn't be further from the truth.

Laughter doesn't cancel your grief. Joy doesn't mean you've stopped loving your spouse. It doesn't mean you've forgotten them. It doesn't mean you've moved on. It simply means you are still alive—and you're honoring that life by letting joy find you again.

My first real moment of joy came about six weeks after Luke died. I took my kids to visit my cousin, who lives on a farm. My daughter Hayley and I ended up milking cows—yes, cows!—and we laughed so hard our stomachs hurt. The boys refused to try, of course, but just watching us had them smiling. My cousin snapped a photo of me mid-laugh and I posted it on Facebook. Later, my aunt that we were staying with said, "It's so good to see your smile and your joy coming back."

Who knew that milking a cow could do that?

Now, I know you're probably not running out to find a cow (though honestly, not the worst idea), but here's the point: sometimes joy sneaks up on us when we're simply living. And that is more than okay. It's necessary.

Over the years, I've heard from hundreds of widows and widowers who've said some version of: "How can I be happy when my spouse just died? It feels wrong."

I get it. It feels strange. Counterintuitive. As if somehow smiling means you're not grieving deeply enough. But staying in a place of constant sorrow doesn't prove your love. It just keeps you stuck.

There's an unspoken belief: the longer you stay sad, the more it proves you loved them. It's a lie.

Your love is not measured by your pain. It lives on in your laughter, too. It lives on in your healing.

Widows often worry how their joy will look to others. "Will they judge me?" Maybe. Maybe not. But we can't live our lives trying to control what people think.

(And yes, I know—that's easier said than done.)

I've been judged plenty. Especially on TikTok, of all places—for smiling or appearing joyful "too soon" after Luke died. But I had to come to this realization: I'm doing what's best for me and my kids. I'm choosing to live. And I'm letting go of what people think.

Did you know that laughter actually helps your brain heal?

Laughter releases endorphins—those "feel-good" chemicals that calm the nervous system and reduce physical tension. It also lowers cortisol, the stress hormone that skyrockets during trauma. Even forced laughter can start a ripple effect of relaxation and emotional release. That's why it's okay—even beneficial—to smile, even when it feels strange.

You are not betraying your spouse by laughing. You are giving your body and soul the space to recover.

10 Ways to Invite Laughter and Joy Back Into Your Life

1. Watch a comedy movie. Start with something familiar. Is there a sitcom, movie, or clip that has always made you laugh?

2. Surround yourself with people who make you laugh. You know the ones—the friends who won't let you stay too serious for too long. Let their laughter soften your grief.

3. Try something silly- Karaoke (have you heard me sing *Summer Lovin'*?), a paint night (you don't even want to see what my paintings look like!), axe throwing (it's harder than it looks!)—yes, even cow milking. Joy often comes in the unexpected when we step outside our regular routines.

4. Start a "Funny Things" journal. Each night, write down one thing that made you smile that day. A meme. Something your kid said. Your dog chasing its tail. Anything. Train your brain to look for joy.

5. Join a widows group focused on fun. Not every group has to be heavy. Look for one that plans game nights, movie nights, or creative meetups. (Our Widow Goals Groups do this all the time!)

6. Filter your social media feed. Unfollow what drags you down. Fill your feed with uplifting, funny, joy-filled content. Let it be a tool for healing, not comparison.

7. Let kids or grandkids pull you into their world. Children are natural joy-givers. Say yes to dancing, dress-up, or letting them paint your face. Their laughter is healing.

8. Say yes to something new. When someone invites you somewhere and it feels safe—say yes. You don't have to be ready. Sometimes, joy shows up when you simply show up.

9. Laugh at the weirdness of grief. Grief is awkward. You'll cry over commercials. Forget what day it is. Talk to the air. Laugh at the absurdity. You're not broken—you're human.

10. Give yourself permission. Say it out loud: "I am allowed to laugh. I am allowed to live. I am allowed to feel joy again." Write it. Frame it. Make it your phone wallpaper. Let this truth sink in.

So, my widow friend, let this be your reminder: God created laughter. He delights in your joy just as much as He holds space for your sorrow. Laughing again doesn't mean you've forgotten your spouse—it means you're embracing the life God still has for you. You can carry grief and joy together. Every time you allow yourself to smile, you are trusting that He is not finished with your story. Let joy be a reflection of your healing and a testimony of God's faithfulness. Your laughter is not a betrayal—it's a beautiful act of worship from a heart that's learning to live again.

Widow Reflections

1. When was the last time you genuinely laughed or smiled? What were you doing? Who were you with? (If you can't remember, that's okay—this is your starting point.)

2. What's one thing that used to bring you joy that you've been hesitant to try again? Could you take one small step toward doing it this week?

3. What would your spouse say about you laughing and living again? How can you honor their memory by embracing life in a new way?

Widow Action Steps

*Say it out loud: "I am allowed to laugh. I am allowed to live. I am allowed to feel joy again."
   *Do one playful thing this week: Try karaoke, a funny movie, or dancing in your kitchen. Let yourself live a little.
   *Start a "Smile File" Write down one thing each day that made you smile or laugh. Let your brain relearn joy.

Goal #11—Take Your Time With Their Things

"There is a time for everything, and a season for every activity under the heavens... a time to keep and a time to throw away." — Ecclesiastes 3:1,6 NIV

Luke's water cup sat half empty on his nightstand. The medications I had placed there the night before—still waiting. And next to them, a plate from the grilled cheese sandwich I had cooked for him the evening before he died. Crumbs were scattered like a trail of heartbreak. I couldn't let anyone touch it. It was like letting go of him all over again. I wasn't ready for that.

His t-shirts still carried the scent of his deodorant. I would press my face into them, trying to breathe in the memory of him, willing the smell to stay forever. I wanted to keep him alive in every way I could—through his scent, his things, the spaces he lived in.

That's the thing no one tells you about grief—how physical it can be. It's not just emotional. It's tangible. You *feel* it in your bones, in your chest, in your hands as you touch their things. A toothbrush becomes sacred. A note scribbled on a napkin feels like a treasure. Even the mess they left behind—dirty socks, a receipt in their wallet—suddenly matters. These items are no longer ordinary; they're the closest connection you have to the person you've lost.

There is no manual for this part of grief. No one prepares you for the moment their shoes become untouchable, or when folding a t-shirt makes you sob. I had to learn the hard way that healing doesn't mean forgetting. And moving forward doesn't mean moving on.

Eventually—weeks, maybe months later—I felt a quiet nudge in my heart. It was time. Not to let go, but to begin. I started small. I opened Luke's drawers, held each item in my hands, and let the memories wash over me. I gave some of his clothes to the kids.

Hayley, especially, had a deep connection to his shirts. When she was little, Luke used to give her one of his t-shirts to sleep in, and she'd call it her "Daddy shirt." She had a sweet habit of asking him for a "fresh one," meaning she wanted a shirt fresh off of him, still warm and smelling like his deodorant. It became their bedtime tradition. Now, even at nineteen, she still wears his shirts to bed and I love it!

After the kids chose what they wanted, I gave a few special items to his mom. The rest I gently folded, and tucked into boxes.

Later that year, I moved homes—and those boxes moved with me. I still haven't gone through all of them. And that's okay.

I have Luke's glasses. His Bibles. His heartfelt homemade cards. Each of the kids now has one of their dad's Bibles, too. I still have three of his prosthetic legs. They're heavy, awkward to store, and yet... I can't bring myself to let them go. Maybe I never will. And again, that's okay.

Here's what I want you to know: there is no right or wrong way to do this. You don't have to clean everything out right away. You don't have to do it all at once. And you absolutely don't have to give away a single thing until *you* are ready.

Some people clean out closets within days—it helps them breathe again. Others wait years because the pain of opening a drawer is just too much. And both responses are perfectly okay. You get to decide what healing looks like for *you*.

Ask yourself these questions:

- Do I feel pressure to do this because of someone else's timeline?

- What would it look like to take one small, manageable step?

- Am I doing this to honor my spouse—or to avoid my pain?

If you're feeling overwhelmed, try this: start with the least emotional things. A stack of old paperwork. Duplicates. Socks. Set a timer for fifteen minutes and stop when it goes off. You're not rushing—you're simply moving at your own pace.

You might want to take photos of items you donate, or write a memory on a card and tape it to something you're keeping. If you're not ready to decide, label a bin "Hold for Later." Be compassionate to yourself in this process.

You are not erasing your spouse by making space. You are not dishonoring them by boxing up their belongings. These aren't just things—they're part of your love story. But remember: your love for them doesn't live in the shirt or the shoes. It lives in you.

And if you're wondering what to do with those sacred items—the wedding ring, the cologne bottle, the favorite hat—here are a few ideas I've heard from other widows and or done myself:

- Turn a favorite shirt into a pillow or quilt

- Give a piece of jewelry to your children on a milestone day

- Keep a small memory box on a shelf or nightstand

- Use one of their Bibles as your devotional and highlight verses you both loved

- Create a shadow box with photos, keys, notes, and mementos

You might keep things you never expected—and let go of things you thought you'd cling to. That's part of the surprise of grief. We don't know what we'll hold on to until the moment comes.

There is beauty in the process, even if it's slow. Even if it's full of tears. Even if you pack the box and open it five years later.

Take your time, friend.
You are not falling behind.
You are not failing.
You are healing.

Widow Reflections

1. What items that belonged to your spouse hold the most emotions for you right now?

2. If you have felt pressure to let go of their things, where is that pressure coming from?

3. What's one way you could honor their memory through something you choose to keep?

Widow Action Steps:

*Choose one item that feels safe and meaningful, journal, pray, or talk to a friend about it.

*Pack a "Not Ready Yet" box and give yourself permission to revisit it in the future—no deadlines.

*Invite a trusted friend to help you go through one small area (only if you want help) and talk about the memories you shared.

Goal #12–Understand Grief Comes in Waves, Not Stages

"When you pass through the waters, I will be with you; and when you pass through the rivers, they will not sweep over you." Isaiah 43:2a NIV

Did you know that the five stages of grief constructed by Dr. Elisabeth Kübler-Ross weren't actually created for people grieving the loss of someone else? These were initially developed for those facing their *own* death.

In her book [1] *On Death and Dying*, Dr. Kübler-Ross shared what she had learned from working with terminally ill patients. She noticed a pattern in how they processed their diagnosis and their mortality. The stages—denial, anger, bargaining, depression, and acceptance—were really about their emotional journey as they faced the reality of dying.

Over time, these stages were widely applied to grieving loved ones, but that wasn't the original intent. In fact, Dr. Kübler-Ross herself later clarified that grief isn't linear and that her model was intended for those dying not those grieving someone who died. Everyone's grief is unique, and there's no right or wrong way to navigate it.

---

1. Kübler-Ross, Elisabeth. On Death and Dying. New York: Scribner, 1969.

While the stages can be helpful as a general framework, it's important to remember they were designed for a completely different experience—the process of coming to terms with your *own* mortality—not the journey of mourning someone you've lost.

Learning this fact was a huge relief. I thought there was something wrong with me because I didn't experience all five stages. I hope this knowledge offers relief for you as well!

Instead of being a set of linear steps, Grief can more accurately be explained as coming in waves: sometimes small, sometimes a tsunami and sometimes a sudden, unexpectedly large one appropriately termed a sneaker wave.

These come at literally any time of day or night. In the beginning, you may feel like you are in a wave pool of endless waves. As you heal, the strength and the quantity of the wave subsides. Eventually, there will be days in between or even months, but as far as I know, there will always be waves.

Another way I've heard grief explained, which really helped me, is something called the "ball in the box" analogy. Imagine your life is a box. Inside the box is a ball—that's your grief—and there's also a small pain button on one side of the box. In the beginning, the grief ball is huge, taking up almost the whole space, and it constantly hits that pain button. It feels like everything hurts, all the time. Over time, the box (your life) gets bigger and the ball shrinks. It doesn't hit the pain button as often, but here's the key: when it does, it still hurts just as much as it did in the beginning. You might go weeks or even months without that ball hitting the button, and then—bam—something random sets it off. It could be a smell, a song, or a place that brings a rush of memories. But just like waves, it doesn't mean you're doing grief "wrong"—it's just how grief works. It still lives inside you, and that's okay.

What do I mean by a wave of grief? This is when something, that could be anything, brings you sadness, not necessarily crying. Here is what is important- don't fight the wave. Don't try to run away from it. Don't try to go over it or under it, the best way is to just go with it and ride the wave.

I have experienced so many random wave griefs over the years, and I am sure you will be able to relate. Here are a few that knocked the wind out of me.

I clearly remember sitting in church a few months after Luke died. While listening to the sermon, my gaze drifted to an elderly couple holding hands. Instantly, tears filled my eyes and I realized once again that I would never grow old with Luke. A few weeks before he died, he was crying, and when I asked him why, he said, "I will never get to meet our grandchildren." That hit me hard. While staring at the older couple in church, I decided to ride the grief wave and let myself feel it. Tears streaming down my face, I couldn't fight it.

I am sure you can relate that a song, a small sound, or just about anything can trigger and take us back to the feeling of being with our late spouse. Another instance actually happened just last week.

For some context, as I write this, it's been five years since Luke's death and two years since I married Joel. One day, Joel wanted to surprise me with a date. He didn't tell me where we were going—we simply got in the car and started driving. We crossed the river from Washington into Oregon, and before I knew it, we were on roads that felt achingly familiar. Roads I hadn't driven in years. Joel couldn't have known, but he was unknowingly taking me along the exact route I used to drive with Luke for his chemotherapy appointments. It was also the path to the medical building where Luke had his port placed just weeks before he died. As we got closer, I grew quiet, the weight of those memories settling over me. A familiar wave of grief washed over me—uninvited but powerful. I didn't fight it. I let it take me where it needed to go. When I explained everything to Joel, he responded with gentle understanding, giving me the space to feel it all and ride the wave for as long as I needed.

I have learned the best thing to do is to really feel the wave by submitting to emotion in that wave, experiencing it, and process-ing it as it strikes you. Sometimes, riding the wave means doing the hard thing even when you are unprepared and exhausted.

I've also noticed that grief waves can come during moments of joy. This might sound strange, but even happy occasions can trigger sadness. When I married Joel, it was one of the happiest days of my life, but it was also bittersweet. There I was in my wedding dress, feeling so much joy, but having some grief because my family would never be whole and complete like it used to be. It's okay to feel a mix of emotions—grief and joy can coexist.

So, what should you do when a wave of grief hits?

First, acknowledge it. Name it for what it is. Then, let yourself feel it.

Don't try to suppress it or push it away. Ride the wave, even if it's uncomfortable.

Sometimes, that means crying it out. Other times, it means sitting quietly with your thoughts or talking to someone you trust. Whatever it looks like for you, just know it's okay.

And here's the thing—the waves will come, but they will also go. They don't last forever, even if it feels that way at the moment. Each wave you ride brings a little more healing and a little more strength. Over time, you'll find that you're stronger than you ever thought you could be. Grief is complicated, but it's also a teacher. It teaches us about love, resilience, and the beauty of memories that can never be taken away.

So when the next wave hits, take a deep breath and ride it. Trust that you'll come out on the other side stronger and more at peace. Remember, you're not alone in this journey. And most importantly, know that God is with you in every wave, offering His comfort and strength.

Widow Reflections

1. Grief as Waves: Think about times when grief has come over you like a wave. Were there any patterns or triggers? How did you respond, and what helped you navigate those moments?

2. Riding the Wave: When grief hits, do you allow yourself to fully feel it, or do you find yourself resisting? What practices could help you embrace your emotions in a healthy way?

3. Grief in Unexpected Moments: Recall a time when grief surfaced unexpectedly. How did you handle it, and what did that experience teach you about your healing journey?

Widow Action Steps

*Schedule a Self-Check-In Day. Choose one day this week to slow down and intentionally ask yourself how you're really doing. Don't wait for a wave—give yourself permission to process whatever emotions come up, even if it's just for 10 minutes.

*Create a Grief Wave Toolkit. Put together a physical or digital "grief wave kit" with comforting items like tissues, a journal, a Bible, a playlist, or a small token that reminds you of peace. Have it ready for when a wave hits unexpectedly.

*Write a Note to Yourself for the Next Wave. In a moment of calm, write a short letter to remind yourself that it's okay to feel deeply. Include truths you want to cling to when it gets hard—like "This won't last forever," or "God is with me in this wave."

Goal #13-Don't Fall for Counterfeit Comfort

"Above all else, guard your heart, for everything you do flows from it."— Proverbs 4:23 NIV

If we try to quickly replace our spouse with another person—or any distraction—we may be able to numb the pain for a while. But what happens when the numbness fades? What happens when our hearts begin to thaw?

That pain often returns with greater intensity, demanding to be felt.

My dear widowed friend, I know the loneliness can be unbearable. I know you miss the sound of your spouse's voice, the feel of their skin, the taste of their lips. You would give anything for just one more night in the arms you thought would hold you forever.

We are especially vulnerable in these moments. That's why we must guard our hearts and put safeguards in place. When we're fragile, it's easy to place our hearts in the wrong hands—too soon, too easily. Distractions are everywhere, offering counterfeit comfort. They appear warm and cozy, like sunshine on your face after days of rain. But they're not real healing.

What Is Counterfeit Comfort?

Counterfeit comfort is anything that tries to take the place of the comfort only God can give. And when we're grieving, there's only One who can meet us in the shattered places—Jesus. Only He can mend the broken cracks in our soul.

Counterfeit comfort comes in many forms. It doesn't look counterfeit at first—it looks inviting. Fun. Even healing. It often takes the shape of something we deeply desire. I know this firsthand. In my early grief, I turned to people instead of God. I started looking to men for attention, companionship, and distraction rather than leaning into God for holy comfort.

After 17 years of marriage, the idea of talking to another man was both terrifying and thrilling. At first, I had no desire to do so—but that changed quickly. One morning, I woke up and decided I wanted to start seeking friendships with men. So, I pursued it. And while there's nothing wrong with desiring companionship, I was trying to fill a God-sized hole with human attention.

There was one friendship in particular that became a problem. It had red flags, but I ignored them. Talking to him helped me forget my pain. He made me feel whole again—for a moment. But when he left, the emptiness returned in full force. I knew God was asking me to let the friendship go. I ignored the prompting—until one night He gave me a dream that left no doubt in my heart. I knew it was time to obey.

With strength only Jesus could provide, I ended that friendship and began to grieve in a healthier way.

Your version of counterfeit comfort may look different. Maybe it's alcohol. Shopping. Food. Maybe it's endlessly scrolling on your phone or staying too busy to stop and feel. But I can promise you this: none of it will truly satisfy. Nothing and no one on this earth can fill a heavenly void.

"Grief has no shortcuts—you have to walk through it. But you're never alone. Jesus walks with you through every painful step."

Instead of letting Jesus fill me daily, I let new friendships become my source of strength. But people can't be saviors. Only Jesus can heal what's broken. Counterfeit comforts eventually collapse under the weight of our pain.

When I finally ended that unhealthy friendship, I returned fully to Jesus. And He was right there, waiting—gentle, loving, and never condemning. He welcomed me back like the good Father He is. I felt peace again.

Now staying connected to God is a priority for me. I protect my heart by having an accountability partner who tells me the truth, even when it's hard to hear. I listen to worship music when I'm tempted to go numb. I use a Bible app every day and try to open it before I open social media. I've learned that what I consume shapes my focus—so I choose wisely.

Early in my grief, I was glued to God. He was my oxygen. I danced in my room to worship music and called Him my husband. But when I drifted from Him and turned toward distractions, I felt the difference immediately. Even then, Jesus didn't give up on me. He kept whispering, "Come back."

And when I did, He embraced me.

This doesn't mean the temptations stopped. Satan is sneaky and relentless. But I've learned that when I keep my communication with God open, I'm far more likely to recognize lies—and more likely to choose truth.

I know some people think God is all rules and restrictions. But His boundaries are born out of love, like a parent warning their toddler away from a hot stove. He sees what we can't. He knows what will harm us—even when we can't yet see it.

Sometimes God gives warnings through dreams. Other times, we need to seek out wisdom in Scripture. Either way, don't ignore His nudges.

One of the best tools I've used to stay on track is Scripture memorization. If you need a starting point, try this one:

"Therefore, since we are surrounded by so great a cloud of witnesses,let us also lay aside every weight, and sin which clings so closely,and let us run with endurance the race that is set before us,looking

to Jesus, *the founder and perfecter of our faith.*"— Hebrews 12:1–2 ESV

Your healing isn't found in distraction—it's found in the arms of the One who knows every broken piece of your heart. When the world shouts for your attention and offers shiny substitutes, remember: you don't need counterfeit comfort. You need the real, lasting love of Jesus. He's not just your healer; He's your steady place, your safe place, your forever comfort. So fix your eyes on Him—not just for today, but for every step of this sacred, messy, beautiful journey called grief. And as you run your race, know you're never running alone.

Widow Reflections

1. What are some areas in your life where you may have sought counterfeit comfort instead of turning to God?

2. What practical steps can you take to guard your heart against distractions and temptations that deter you away from true healing?

3. How does the truth of God's love and guidance provide a deeper, more lasting comfort than the temporary relief counterfeit comforts offer?

Widow Action Steps

*Identify and Release Counterfeit Comforts- Spend time in prayer or journaling to recognize anything or anyone you've turned to for comfort instead of God. Ask Him to gently remove what doesn't belong and to fill those spaces with His peace.

*Invite Accountability- choose one trusted friend to help keep you grounded. Let them know the areas where you're most vulnerable and ask them to lovingly check in with you regularly.

*Start Your Day with Jesus- before turning to your phone or daily tasks, take five minutes each morning to pray, read a verse, or listen to a worship song. Let Him be your first source of comfort and strength.

Goal #14 – Give Back to Others

"H e comforts us in all our troubles so that we can comfort others. When they are troubled, we will be able to give them the same comfort God has given us." 2 Corinthians 1:4 NLT

If you are earlier in your grief—a phase I call being a *baby widow*—and feel like you're barely surviving, then you may not be ready for this chapter. That's okay. Come back when the timing feels right.

But if you're beginning to see glimpses of strength return, one of the best ways to keep moving forward is by giving to others. I know what you're thinking—you don't have the time, the energy, or even the bandwidth to help someone else. But hear me out.

When we step outside of our own pain, even momentarily, and pour into someone else, something begins to shift. It's not just a warm, fuzzy feeling—it's actually backed by science. Studies consistently show that helping others reduces stress, anxiety, and depression while increasing overall well-being.

A review published in *BMC Public Health* found that people who volunteer tend to have better mental health and lower rates of depression (Jenkinson et al., 2013). Another study in *Social Science & Medicine* revealed that regular volunteers experience greater life satisfaction and lower stress levels (Meier & Stutzer, 2008).

Have you ever done something kind for someone and felt an unexpected boost of joy? That's because giving activates the brain's reward system, releasing feel-good chemicals like endorphins and oxytocin—similar to a runner's high.

Grief often robs us of our sense of purpose. But giving back, even in small ways, can begin to restore that purpose. According to *The Journal of Positive Psychology*, people who perform acts of kindness report higher levels of fulfillment and life purpose (Van Tongeren et al., 2016).

Even neuroscience confirms it—serving others activates the prefrontal cortex, which helps regulate emotions and reduce negative thought patterns (JAMA *Psychiatry*, 2015). In simple terms, giving to others doesn't just help them—it rewires your brain for healing.

When you're grieving, the idea of giving back might feel overwhelming. I get it. You're just trying to survive. But one of the most healing things you can do is step outside of your own pain—even for a moment—and give to someone else. It doesn't have to be big or complicated. Even small acts of kindness can create a ripple effect, not just in their life, but in yours too.

Ways Widows Can Give Back

1. Encourage Another Widow- No one understands this journey like another widow. If you've been walking this path for a while, reach out to someone who is newly widowed. A simple text, a coffee date, or just listening can mean everything to someone who feels lost. Sometimes, just knowing they're not alone is the greatest gift you can give.

2. Lead a Widow Goals Group- One of the best ways to give back is by helping other widows not only survive but thrive. If you've gained wisdom and strength through your own journey, consider leading a Widow Goals group. This is a powerful way to create a safe, encouraging space where widows can support one another, set goals, and move forward with hope. By guiding others through this process, you'll help others heal while continuing your own healing.

(link in back of book to apply)

3. Volunteer Your Time- When you're ready, consider volunteering for a cause that resonates with your heart. Maybe it's serving at a grief support group, a local shelter, or an organization that mattered to your spouse. Giving even an hour of your time can bring a deep sense of purpose and connection.

4. Share Your Story- Your story has power. Whether it's through a blog, social media, a podcast, or speaking at a support group, sharing your journey can encourage others who feel like they'll never make it through. You never know who needs to hear your words. You can also share your story on my podcast *Widowed 2 Soon!* (link in back of book to apply)

5. Write a Letter or Send a Care Package- Think about a widow who might be struggling. Maybe it's someone you know personally or someone you've seen in a support group. Sending a handwritten note, a small care package, or even a book that helped you through can be a tangible way to show love and support.

6. Support a Cause in Their Honor- Many widows find healing in doing something in honor of their late spouse. Whether it's organizing a fundraiser, walking in a charity event, or donating to a cause they cared about, giving back in their name can turn pain into purpose.

7. Offer Practical Help- Sometimes, the best way to give is through simple, everyday acts. Help a single mom who's overwhelmed, bring a meal to someone who's struggling, or babysit for a friend who needs a break. Sometimes, just showing up for someone else helps remind us that we still

have something to give.

Giving back doesn't mean you have to be "healed" or have it all figured out. It just means taking what you've been through and using it to lift someone else up. And the beautiful thing? In doing so, you'll find healing, too.

Grief has a way of making us feel stuck—like we're trapped in our own pain, unable to see beyond the weight of loss. But one of the most powerful ways to begin healing is to step outside of ourselves and give to others. It doesn't erase the pain, but it gives it purpose.

Whether it's encouraging another widow, volunteering, sharing your story, or leading a *Widow Goals* group, these acts of kindness create ripples that reach far beyond what we can see. When we give, we're reminded that we still have something valuable to offer—that our story, our journey, and our hearts can still bring hope to others.

But here's the beautiful truth: giving back isn't just for them. It's for us, too. Every time we extend a hand to help someone else, we take another step forward in our own healing. We shift our focus from what we've lost to what we can still give. We begin to rebuild not just our lives, but the lives of those around us.

God doesn't waste our pain. The comfort He gives us in our hardest moments isn't meant to stay with us—it's meant to be shared. And as we comfort others, we find that our own hearts begin to heal in ways we never expected.

So, if you feel like you have nothing left to give, start small. A kind word. A listening ear. A moment of encouragement. And watch as those small moments turn into something far greater than you ever imagined.

Healing doesn't happen in isolation. It happens in community. And when we walk this journey together, we don't just survive—we thrive.

Widow Reflections

1. Reflect on a time when helping someone else brought you healing or joy. How did that experience shape your grief journey?

2. Consider the giving-back ideas mentioned in this chapter. Which one speaks to you the most and why?

3. Meditate on 2 Corinthians 1:4: "*He comforts us in all our troubles so that we can comfort others.*" How has God's comfort shown up in your life? In what ways might He be calling you to extend that comfort to someone else?

Widow Action Steps

*Write down one simple way you could give back this week—even if it's as small as sending a text to another widow.

*Make a list of people or causes that matter to you. Which one could you support in memory of your spouse or in alignment with your healing journey?

*Choose one of the "Ways Widows Can Give Back" and commit to trying it this month. Don't wait to feel ready—just start where you are.

Goal #15- Discover Your Purpose

"**F**or we are God's handiwork, created in Christ Jesus to do good works, which God prepared in advance for us to do." Ephesians 2:10 NIV

What if your deepest pain could point you toward your greatest purpose?

Let's talk about purpose. Purpose is what gets you up in the morning. It's what keeps you going when nothing else makes sense. And no, I'm not necessarily talking about a job—though the dream is that your purpose and your career collide. Purpose is God's calling on your life. It's the fire inside of you that burns quietly at first, then begins to roar when you step into what you were created to do.

In the beginning of your widow journey, your purpose might just be surviving—and that's okay. If getting out of bed and brushing your teeth is all you can do today, that is your purpose for now. Give yourself grace. This chapter will be waiting when you're ready for more.

Eventually, the fog begins to lift. The question, "*What's next for me?*" starts to float in. That's when you know—it's time to take the next step.

I remember a few months after Luke died, I imagined my future like a blank, wordless book. It was terrifying... and freeing. I could write anything I wanted. But I had no idea what to write.

As a child, I always knew I wanted to be a mom and a teacher. I pursued that dream with a master's degree in education. But truthfully? I never got to fully enjoy it. During my second year of teaching, Luke was diagnosed with cancer. Life changed overnight.

I was pulled in a thousand directions—wife, mother, caregiver, teacher. I admired teachers who poured their hearts into their classrooms. But for me, teaching became something I had to do, not something I was truly called to.

I had also dreamed of being a stay-at-home mom. That dream didn't unfold either. I returned to full-time work when Hayden was just six weeks old because Luke was still recovering from his amputation and the effects of chemo. It broke me. Every morning I left him crying, I cried too. I pumped milk in a school bathroom while trying to hold my life together. I watched the moms of my students walk in wearing workout clothes and talking about brunch plans—and I desperately wanted that freedom.

Instead, I was 25 years old, navigating my husband's cancer diagnosis and a life I hadn't signed up for.

After Luke died, I tried going back to teaching at a few different schools. But I felt it in my bones—my purpose had shifted. I had experienced healing that I couldn't keep to myself. I wanted to help other widows find that healing, too.

And so, a new calling began to stir.

It started small. I created a TikTok account (@widowgoals) and posted encouraging (and slightly cringey) videos. Some of those early ones still make me laugh—and not in a proud way. But they were my baby steps into ministry. If you really want a laugh, scroll to the beginning and watch me dance on countertops. (Yes, that happened.)

To my surprise, people started messaging me. *"Thank you." "I thought I was alone." "Your videos are helping me."* That's when I realized—this wasn't just content. This was *connection*. This was *purpose*.

Next came the *Widowed 2 Soon* podcast, which I launched with a widower friend. I was still less than a year into my own grief, but I found healing in helping others heal. The podcast grew and evolved, and now, four years later, it's still going strong.

That podcast opened the door to starting my nonprofit, *Widow Goals*. Today, support groups are meeting across the globe—bringing hope, encouragement, and healing to people who never thought they'd smile again.

I'm not telling you all this to brag. I'm telling you this because *this all started with one small step*. I had no roadmap. I didn't even feel fully healed. But I was willing to move forward.

You may be reading this thinking, "That's great for you, Michelle, but I have no idea what I'm supposed to do." I get it. I was once in that place too. But here's what I know: God has a purpose for you, and it's bigger than you can even imagine.

How to Begin Discovering Your Purpose

- If time and money weren't a factor, what would you do with your days?

- What lights you up inside? What topic could you talk about for hours and never grow tired?

- What are your gifts and hobbies? Your purpose often hides in the things you already love.

- Ask your people. Sometimes, friends and family see something in us we don't see in ourselves.

- And most importantly, pray. Ask God to reveal your next step. Listen for the gentle nudge, the whisper that doesn't go away.

Remember, purpose doesn't always arrive with fanfare. Sometimes it comes quietly—through a conversation, a volunteer moment, or even a TikTok dance video. Wherever you are, take the next small step. You don't need to know the whole plan. Just follow the pull on your heart.

You are here for a reason. God didn't bring you this far to leave you in the dark. Your story isn't over. There is purpose in your pain—and it's being written even now.

Widow Reflections

1. Reflecting on Purpose: How has your own understanding of purpose shifted throughout different seasons of your life?

2. Passion & Calling: If time and money were not a factor, what would you spend your time doing? How does this align (or not align) with what you feel called to do?

3. What is one small step you could take today to explore or move toward your purpose?

Widow Action Steps

*Take out a journal and list what brings you joy, what you're passionate about, what others say you're good at, and what activities make you feel most alive. Look for patterns—your purpose often hides in the overlap.

*Sign up for a class, volunteer, start a blog, or share a piece of your story online. You don't need to have it all figured out. Just take one step in the direction that excites or intrigues you.

*Spend time in prayer this week specifically asking God to show you your purpose and give you the courage to walk in it. Keep a notebook nearby to jot down any ideas, nudges, or dreams that come to mind.

Goal #16 – Let Go of Guilt

"**I**t is for freedom that Christ has set us free. Stand firm, then, and do not let yourselves be burdened again by a yoke of slavery." Galatians 5:1 NIV

Guilt — a concept that is specifically hard for widows. Experiencing guilt over living life again is not a burden you are meant to carry. My counselor taught me that every thought we have originates from God, self, or Satan. We know God wouldn't put that guilt on you, so it is either you or Satan giving you those thoughts.

Why do so many widows feel guilt? The circumstances may differ, but the lies often sound the same:

"I feel guilty because I never said this, or never did that."

"I wish I could go back in time and change things."

I hear you. I've been there.

After Luke died, guilt wrapped itself around me like a blanket. One of my deepest regrets is that we left the house too quickly. The hospice nurse suggested we go right away so the kids wouldn't see the coroner. I was trying to protect them, but in doing so, I lost a moment I can never get back—I didn't kiss him goodbye.

I didn't even know the coroner had been called until it was already in motion. Everything happened so fast. I watched the kids say their goodbyes, each kissing their father for the last time, while I held back the tidal wave rising inside me.

After they left, I crawled into bed with him one last time, as I had thousands of times before, but this time, he wasn't there. His body was there, but his soul was gone. The soul that I loved deeply, the soul that I dreamed with, cried with, laughed with, and the soul that I knew was now with Jesus. All the anguish I had been holding in cascaded out of me. I began to wail from a deeper pain than I had known was possible. I knew that he was gone, but I just couldn't comprehend it. How could the man I had shared life with for the past 18 years be gone in an instant?

My mom tried to console me as my sobs shook the bed. Then I heard they were on their way to take his body, and panic set in. I scrambled to gather the kids, give the dog to a neighbor, and do whatever I could to shield them from more pain. But later, the realization hit me like a wave: I never kissed him goodbye. We had always kissed goodbye—always. So how could I have forgotten the final time?

Guilt manifested:
Regret
An awful pit in my stomach
Desperately wanting to rewind the clock
and change things
A domino effect of regrets occurred:
regrets of time spent away..
regrets over stupid arguments
regrets of unsaid conversations
and so many more.

When I recall that day, I remind myself: I was in shock. I was trying to protect my children. I was walking through something I had never experienced before. And just like you, I did the best I could in an impossible moment.

You don't have to carry guilt as a punishment for loving deeply and losing painfully. You don't have to keep reliving the moments you wish had gone differently. You can honor your spouse, love them forever, and still let go of the guilt. Over time, I have learned the tools to let go of regrets, and so can you.

When we have regrets, it is like carrying a heavy weight around our necks—a weight that is too much for us to humanly carry. We need to release those regrets. There are a few practical ways that have helped me.

One of the most impactful things I did was write a letter to Luke. I apologized for the things I had done wrong in our marriage, and I even apologized for not kissing him goodbye. I forgave him for the things he did that hurt me over the years, and I told him anything and everything else that I wanted to. Then I took a bold step and read it aloud to a trusted person. I said goodbye—not to Luke, but to the pain caused by my regrets and unfinished pain.

It wasn't a magic formula, but I felt such a sense of relief being able to talk about all the things that were once hidden. Did you know that things in the dark lose their power over us when we bring them into the light? I encourage you to write a similar letter.

Another approach when I can't carry something anymore is to surrender it to God. He's big enough to hold our regret, strong enough to carry our guilt, and kind enough to respond with grace. If you're not sure what to pray, try this:

"God, I don't know how to let go of this. I keep replaying it, and it hurts. Please help me see this memory through Your eyes. Help me believe that Your grace covers even this."

And then just sit in that moment. Let peace meet you right where you are. God will cover you with the peace that passes all understanding as you lean into Him.

Let's talk about something that no one warns you about after your spouse dies: survivor's guilt. It's that quiet, painful question that creeps in when the world keeps spinning and you're somehow still here... and they're not.

It sounds like: "Why am I still alive and they're not?" "Why did I get more time with the kids, and my spouse didn't?" "Why am I planning birthday parties, going to weddings, laughing with friends... while my spouse is missing the experience?

It's a guilt that whispers you don't deserve to keep living when the person you loved most doesn't get that opportunity. It can show up in the most unexpected moments. A vacation. A milestone. Even a random Tuesday when the sun feels too bright for the weight you're carrying inside.

Here's what I've learned: you don't honor the person you lost by shrinking your life to match their death.

You honor them by fully living the life you still have.

Survivor's guilt is a liar. It tells you that because they didn't get more time, you shouldn't enjoy the time you've been given. But that's not the truth. That's not grace. And that's not from God.

God is not asking you to feel guilty for surviving. He's asking you to trust that He still has purpose for your life—even in the middle of the pain. Even when you don't understand it. Even when you would trade places in a heartbeat.

You are still here because your story isn't finished yet.

My dear widowed brothers and sisters, If you are carrying survivor's guilt, let me remind you: You didn't choose this. You didn't choose to be the one still living, but here you are. You are still here for a reason. You are chosen. And God has a plan for you—a plan far bigger than either of us can comprehend.

You get to love fiercely. You get to show up for your family. You get to laugh again, cry again, dance again, and dream again. You get to become the new version of yourself that God is lovingly molding you into. You get to honor their memory by living boldly.

Their death doesn't mean your life has to end, too.

It's okay to feel joy. It's okay to move forward. It's okay to live fully. And it's okay to do it all while still loving them deeply.

Because love doesn't die. And neither does purpose.

You are allowed to be here. You are meant to be here. And friend, you don't need to apologize for surviving.

So what do we do when the guilt creeps in? We release it once again. Through writing, praying, journaling, and talking with a trusted friend. We realize that guilt is a feeling and not a fact. Our feelings and emotions can easily lie to us.

Your regrets do not define you. Releasing them will most likely be something you do more than once, but I pray that through this process you will be able to live in freedom. It is for freedom that Christ has set us free! We need to really believe and live that.

Guilt is heavy—but you don't have to carry it anymore. Whether it's regrets over what you said or didn't say, things you wish you had done differently, or simply the ache of still being here when they're not...I challenge you to release it. You are not alone in these feelings, and you are not broken because you have them. But God never intended for you to live weighed down by guilt. He came to bring freedom, and that freedom includes you, right here, right now.

So, take a deep breath. Write the letter. Say the prayer. Share your story. And little by little, let God replace your guilt with His grace. You are still here because your story isn't finished yet. Choose to live it fully without guilt, and with the beautiful peace that comes when you finally let go.

Widow Reflections

1. What regrets or moments of guilt have I been carrying, and how have these impacted my ability to move forward in healing?

2. If I could see my story through God's eyes, how might He speak to the parts of me still stuck in guilt or shame?

3. What is one step I can take this week to begin releasing guilt—whether through writing, prayer, or a conversation with someone I trust?

Widow Action Steps

*Write a letter to your spouse expressing any regrets, apologies, or unspoken words. Consider reading it aloud to a trusted friend or counselor to release what's been trapped inside.

*Pray through your guilt, asking God to help you see your situation through His eyes and to replace guilt with His grace and truth.

*Choose one moment this week—a joyful event, a walk outside, or even a meal you enjoy—and intentionally allow yourself to fully experience it without guilt.

Goal #17– Face Loneliness with Faith and Courage

"**F**ear not, for I am with you; be not dismayed, for I am your God. I will strengthen you, I will help you, I will uphold you with my righteous right hand." Isaiah 41:10 ESV

What does it really mean to feel lonely?

Loneliness isn't just about being alone. You can be in a crowded room and still feel completely isolated. Some of my most profound moments of loneliness as a widow happened when I was surrounded by people. Strangely, church was one of the hardest places. I'd look around and see families sitting together, smiling, holding hands. Watching a young girl rest her head on her father's shoulder still brings a sharp ache to my heart.

In fact, just last week at church, I witnessed a moment that brought that ache rushing back. A little girl, maybe around seven or eight, climbed up into her daddy's arms. And just like that, my heart broke all over again—for my daughter, for what she lost, for what can never be replaced.

On a trip to the beach not long after Luke passed, I found myself staring at an elderly couple walking along the shoreline. Their hands were clasped, their bare feet sinking into the wet sand with each quiet step. Every so often, one would lean in to whisper something, and the other would smile. They moved in unspoken rhythm, like they had spent a lifetime learning each other's pace. A lump rose in my throat. Luke and I would never be that couple.

We would never grow old together, never take slow walks in the sand after years of shared memories. The oldest we ever got to be together was 41 and 42. He will forever be 42.

Over the years, working with widows from all walks of life, I've learned that loneliness comes in many forms. There are so many different circumstances that can intensify it.

When Luke died, my kids were 12, 14, and 15. In one way, it was incredibly difficult. I was not only grieving my own loss but also carrying the weight of their grief. I was a mom trying to stay strong while mourning the love of my life and aching for my kids, who had lost their dad—an experience I had never personally known.

But in another way, I was so thankful to have my kids at home. I wasn't living alone, and that was a gift.

The first few nights after Luke died, we had extended family staying with us. But the night everyone left, and it was just the four of us at home, the emptiness was deafening. I walked around the house, overwhelmed by the gaping hole his absence left behind.

Though four of us still lived within those same 1,446 square feet, the silence screamed louder than words ever could. In all our years of marriage, I had only spent one night in that house without him—and that was when he was receiving chemotherapy, and I was very pregnant with our oldest son. Even then, I only left to get the rest I desperately needed. Our kids had never known a night without him at home.

Maybe your story is different. Maybe your kids are grown and out of the house, or perhaps you never had children. You may be facing the quiet of a home where you are physically alone, and that's a very hard adjustment.

I want you to know I see you, I understand you, and I'm praying for you. I pray God meets you in your loneliness—whether you are secluded and without a companion, or in a crowded space where the contrast reminds you of your loss.

For many widows, nights are the hardest. Nearly every widow I've spoken to agrees—the darkness seems to magnify the emptiness. The cold, empty side of the bed is a harsh reminder of the life we no longer have. My mind wouldn't rest, and I often cried myself to sleep, my heart shattered and aching.

No matter your situation, loneliness is something we all encounter. So how do we deal with it? How do we keep showing up in a world where our other half is missing?

Some try to fill the void with distractions—TV, social media, shopping, food. Anything to numb the pain. And while those things may offer temporary relief, they won't fill the emptiness inside.

I've discovered that the only true comfort—the only lasting peace—comes from God. There were countless times I cried out to Him—sometimes with my hands raised high, begging Him to stop the pain, and other times face down on the floor, pleading with Him to fill the gaping void in my heart.

And you know what? He always showed up. He still does.

There's a peace I can't explain—one that wraps around me like a soft blanket. It's the kind of peace that doesn't make sense in the natural, and yet it calms every storm within me.

If you've never experienced that kind of peace, I encourage you to ask God to meet you in that place. Turn on worship music. (If you don't know what to play, just say what I do and say: "Alexa, play worship music.") Close your eyes. Take deep breaths. Let His presence wash over you. He's not far—He's closer than you think.

And while God is enough, I also know we were created for connection. We were not made to do life alone. Be sure to read Chapter 6 for practical tips on surrounding yourself with others.

In the meantime, here are a few ideas to help you combat loneliness in a healthy way:

Ideas to Help with Loneliness

- Start a daily connection habit. Text or call one friend every day, even if it's just to say hello. Small interactions matter.

- Join a group—online or in person. Whether it's a grief group, book club, Bible study, or fitness class, being around others helps fill that social void.

- Volunteer. Helping others is one of the fastest ways to shift your focus from pain to purpose. Find a cause that speaks to your heart.

- Create a "comfort corner" in your home. A cozy chair, your Bible, a journal, and a soft blanket. Let this be your go-to space for peace and connection with God.

- Talk to a counselor or coach. Sometimes, having someone to help you process your grief is incredibly healing.

- Adopt a pet. If it fits your lifestyle, animals offer beautiful companionship. A wagging tail or a purring cat can ease the ache of an empty home.

- Practice gratitude. Each night, write down three things you're thankful for. Gratitude shifts the atmosphere—even on the darkest days.

Loneliness can feel like a tidal wave—unexpected, overwhelming, and relentless. But hear me when I say this: it won't always feel this heavy. I know we may have never met in person, but I want you to know—from one widow to another—I am here for you. I understand the depth of the loneliness you're walking through.

And sweet friend, you are not alone. You have me. You have a whole community of widows who truly get it. (If you're looking for connection, I invite you to join our *Widowed 2 Soon* Community on Facebook—we would love to welcome you with open arms.)

And most importantly, you have the God of the universe walking beside you.

He sees every tear. He hears every silent cry. He gathers your tears in a bottle and holds your broken heart gently in His hands. He weeps with you. And He loves you more than you could ever imagine.

God is not distant. He is not unaware. He sees you, hears you, and walks beside you in your loneliest hours. You are not forgotten. You are not forsaken. You are deeply loved.

And with His presence in your life, you can face even the loneliest nights—with faith, and with courage.

Widow Reflections

1. When do you feel the most lonely, and what do you usually do in those moments? Take a moment to reflect on what your patterns are and whether they bring comfort or just distraction. Is there a new way you could invite God or others into that space?

2. Have you experienced the peace of God in your loneliness? If so, what did it feel like? If not, would you be willing to ask Him to meet you there?

3. What is one small step you could take this week to connect—with God, with someone else, or with your own heart? Think of something simple and doable: sending a text, joining a group, creating a quiet space for prayer, or even just stepping outside for a walk and talking to God.

Widow Action Steps

*Identify your loneliness triggers. Write down specific moments or environments when loneliness hits hardest. Awareness will help you respond with intention instead of just reacting.

*Invite God into one lonely moment this week. Whether it's through worship music, journaling, or simply sitting in silence and talking to Him, take time to intentionally welcome His presence into your pain.

*Reach out to one person. Send a text, make a phone call, or join a group. Just one small connection can begin to shift your sense of isolation into a sense of belonging.

Goal #18–Learn How to Be a Solo Parent

"**H**e tends his flock like a shepherd: He gathers the lambs in his arms and carries them close to his heart; he gently leads those that have young." Isaiah 40:11 NIV

If you don't have kids, feel free to skip this chapter.

There is a big difference between a single parent and a solo parent. I used to say I was a single parent until I learned the difference. A single parent has another parent with whom to share responsibilities. The kids usually spend some days out of the home. Of great contrast, the single parent is not dealing with the grief of the kids with the death of the other parent.

Solo parents are really solo in every sense of the word. Suddenly, all decisions for your children are wholly your responsibility because you are alone in this role.

I remember being so deep in my own grief, yet having to also carry the grief of my kids. It was an almost impossible daily task. Everyone's experience is different, but this was mine.

My kids were 12, 14, and almost 16 at the time of Luke's death. We all know those ages are hard enough without throwing in death and grief, and for my kids, this was intensified because of years of watching their dad be sick. They each handled grief in their own unique ways.

Payton, my 12-year-old at the time, didn't talk much about his grief. He buried himself in typical tween activities and rarely opened up. After many gentle nudges, he finally agreed to see a counselor—but only once. He hated it. (Ironically, now at 17, he loves going to counseling and tries to go as often as possible!)

My 14-year-old daughter Hayley took on a mother-like role to her brothers and even me. She recently revealed to me (she is 19 now) that she felt like she had to be everyone's mother, even me! At the time, I was just barely surviving, so I had no idea she was experiencing the need to bear such a heavy burden. But she said I was crying so much that she had to be the one to mother everyone. She was more open with me about her feelings—as girls often are—but she still held a lot of grief in.

My oldest son, Hayden, was just shy of 16 when Luke passed, and like many grieving teens, he didn't know how to process the tidal wave of emotions. I noticed him trying to step into a role he was never meant to carry. People told him he was now the "man of the house," and while I know they meant well, those words placed an unfair burden on his young shoulders. His grief showed up in ways that were hard to handle—through conflict, deflection, and pushing boundaries. We had some very difficult days. But I held on to hope, prayed continually, and reached out for help when I needed it. Today, he's a young adult who has grown so much, and I'm incredibly proud of how far he's come.

While my children were in their tween and teen years when Luke died, I've walked alongside many widows with young children, and I want to acknowledge the unique challenges that come with parenting little ones in grief.

When your kids are young, you may not be navigating teenage pushback or existential questions, but you're likely fielding constant needs with very few breaks. You're answering innocent yet heartbreaking questions like, "When is Daddy coming back from Heaven?" or "Who's going to tuck me in now?" And in the moments you most want to curl up in bed and shut out the world, you might have a toddler needing a snack, a diaper change, or a favorite stuffed animal found right now.

Young children often grieve in short bursts—they may cry one moment and play the next, which can be confusing if you're still stuck in the depths of adult sorrow. But their hearts are grieving, too. You might see regression in potty training, trouble sleeping, separation anxiety, or tantrums that seem to come out of nowhere. These are all ways young children express grief without words.

One widow shared that after her husband died, her 4-year-old began crawling into bed every night, needing the security of closeness. She was so exhausted but chose to let those nights be moments of bonding rather than interruptions. She whispered prayers into her child's hair and held space for both of their broken hearts.

If this is you, I encourage you: snuggle longer, explain gently, cry in front of them, and let them cry in front of you. It's okay to say "I don't know" when they ask the hard questions. It's okay to say, "I miss Daddy too." You don't need perfect answers—you just need to be present.

Your little ones may not remember every detail of this season, but they will remember how safe they felt with you. They will remember the routines you created, the silly moments you made happen, and the way you loved them fiercely through your own tears.

I think what was most difficult was grieving two separate relationships. I grieved the loss of my husband and also the loss of my children's father. I grieved for the relationship I had with Luke and grieved for my kids as I watched their hearts break daily for their dad.

I hated every decision that now had to be made on my own. I realized that there was no one else left on Earth who loved my kids as much as me—no more help with all the parenting responsibilities, no one to help with driving, cooking, cleaning, no one with whom to share a safe place to talk about my kids with someone equally as invested. I began to feel so very alone. The one who gave me these children was no longer there to help. In this place, which felt isolating, I felt the heavy weight of grief and overwhelming responsibility, without Luke to bounce ideas off of or laugh at the silly things the kids do.

So, years into this journey, how have I survived as a solo parent? I survived one day at a time and with a lot of prayers! In my case, my husband was sick for years, so I had already been doing much of the parenting on my own, but not having him there to talk to was excruciating.

It is important as a solo parent to have open and honest conversations with your kids appropriate to their specific age. Share with them that you're having a hard time too; one of the worst things we can do is put on a false face for our kids, as we often believe the lie that we must be strong for them. They need to see us cry so they know it's okay for them to cry too. Create a safe environment for them to talk about their parent. We still often say, "Daddy would have loved this," or "What do you think Daddy would have thought about this?" Let it be normal for their name to be spoken daily. Don't shy away from your kid's emotions. Lean into what they are feeling. Put away the phone and distractions, and just listen. Sometimes, that is all they need. Don't automatically try to fix them. Let them just be. For what we feel, God can heal.

Even though life is chaotic when your spouse dies, for the sake of the kids, please try to keep some kind of routine. When everything else in their world has been turned upside down, your kids need to have some sense of normalcy. Try to resume some of the routines established before the death of their parent. If you didn't have a routine due to sickness, establish a new one, even if it's just a few simple things they can count on.

Maybe you do something specific in the morning or a family activity in the evening. When Luke was very sick and nearing his death, the kids were home from school due to COVID, so we stayed up late every night. We had popcorn and watched a movie or a show. After he died, we continued that tradition, and although there was a massive emptiness in his recliner, my kids and I loved continuing this comforting routine. Hopefully, yours is a healthier routine, but I hope there is something you can all embrace and lean into that brings comfort and security.

Also, have something to look forward to every day, both for yourself and the kids. It may be going to a favorite restaurant, the park, game night, or the movies, but help your family have events and times that bring them joy.

As you navigate this new world as a solo parent, don't be afraid to enlist others to help you. Remember, so many people want to help, but they simply don't know what to do. I had to ask others for rides so many times for my kids when I had to be in multiple locations or when I had to work, and they needed to be somewhere. Create a group chat with friends who have offered to help with rides, and send a text when you need assistance. You are not a burden and it will most likely help your friends feel useful because they are physically doing something to support you.

Finding community again takes effort, but it's so worth it. Look for widow support groups, solo parenting groups, or single parent communities—whether in person through a local church or online on platforms like Facebook. In the beginning, you might feel most comfortable connecting only with others who have also lost a spouse, and that's completely okay. As time goes on, you may feel ready to be in spaces with people who are divorced or chose single parenting. Trust your pace.

Churches can be a great resource, even if you don't share their exact beliefs. Many host groups simply as a way to serve the community, without expecting you to become a member or agree with everything they believe. The important thing is finding a safe, supportive space where you feel seen and less alone.

Have you ever been on a plane and heard that you should put on your own oxygen mask before putting on the masks of those around you, specifically your kids? Well, the same is true in your new journey as a widow and solo parent. What does that mean for you? It means taking care of your mental and physical health so that you can be the best parent possible to your children. Remember, you are the only one they have left, and they need the healthiest version of you.

For me, that meant continuing to run—because during those runs, I felt God's presence more clearly than anywhere else. I also made it a priority to connect with at least two friends each week. Whether it was a walk, coffee, or lunch, those simple moments helped nourish both my soul and my relationships.

I also took up a new hobby, line dancing. There were three of us widows, and sometimes more, who would get to boot scootin' every week or as much as our schedules would allow. This new hobby allowed me to feel joy again. In those moments on the dance floor, the pain of Luke's death seemed a million miles away.

In contrast, it is also important to let yourself really feel your feelings. If we stuff them, we never deal with them and can't move forward in our lives. There is a balance between getting out and doing things and letting ourselves feel. We need a balance of both.

I also love a good, hot, bubbly bath-bombed soak at the end of a long day. Some of my most honest prayers have been spoken in the tub. It's one of those sacred, quiet spaces where I pour out my heart to God, because He meets us anywhere—even in the middle of bath time.

And speaking of talking to God—that has been the single most powerful lifeline for me as a widow and solo parent. No matter where you are or what you're facing, the best thing you can do is keep that line of communication open with the One who under-stands it all.

I had a widower friend who shared that every time he drove, he would imagine Jesus sitting with him in the front seat and conversing. I started doing that, and it was incredible how close God felt to me. I also implemented walks with Jesus as much as I could. On these walks, I would purposely leave my phone at home and, just like in the car, envision Jesus walking beside me. No topics were off limits. There were times I just cried and angrily asked, "Why?" Sometimes I shouted, sometimes I whispered, but in this sacred space, I allowed myself to just be me. No one judging me, and no one needs me. Just me and my creator alone in the depths of my pain, my sorrow, my broken heart, and my questions: Why? My fears about the future, the pain of watching my children grow up without their dad, and the endless cycle of wondering why and how this was my life. Not one of my friends from high school or college was widowed. I felt so alone, but those walks, those talks were like water for my thirsty heart. Jesus became the very air I breathed. I knew I couldn't survive one moment without Him.

I hope you, too, can have this intimate experience with our Savior. He sees you, He feels your pain, and He literally weeps with you.

"*You keep track of all my sorrows. You have collected all my tears in your bottle. You have recorded each one in your book.*" Psalm 56:8 NLT

Run to Him, curl up in His lap, and let Him wipe away your tears. Let Him be the co-parent to your kids. He loves your kids as much as you do—and even more! It is hard to imagine anyone loving them more than you do, but He does! Ask Him to help you parent, and He will meet you there. He tells us that if we lack the knowledge to ask Him, He will give it to us. I have asked Him so many times in my solo parent journey for wisdom, and He always does. Sometimes, the answer comes from another person, a thought I have, the Bible, or any creative way that He chooses to speak to me.

Solo parenting through grief is hands down one of the hardest things I've ever faced—but I want you to know, you don't have to face it alone. God is walking this road with you. He sees every tear, hears every late-night prayer, and shows up in the smallest, most unexpected ways. You're not expected to have it all figured out. Just keep showing up for your kids the best you can—with your beautifully broken, brave heart. Keep leaning on Jesus. Keep asking for help. And know this: even on the days you feel like a mess, you are still enough. With God as your co-parent, you are never truly doing this solo.

Widow Reflections

1. What steps can you take to balance your own grief while supporting your children in processing theirs?

2. How can you establish or maintain routines that provide stability and comfort for your children in the midst of change?

3. In what ways can you enlist help from your community, friends, or church to lighten the load of solo parenting?

4. Bonus Reflection (for moms with little ones): What are your children's emotional and physical needs right now, and how can you gently support them—even in your grief?

Widow Action Steps

*Take time to grieve alongside your children. Let your kids see your emotions so they know it's safe to share theirs. Create a space where all feelings are welcome and nothing is off limits.

*Establish one consistent routine this week. Whether it's morning snuggles, movie night, or a walk around the block—build a rhythm that your kids can rely on. Stability brings security.

*Make a list of 3 people you can ask for help. Reach out to one this week. Whether it's a ride, a meal, or just someone to listen—you don't have to do this alone. Community matters.

*Bonus Action Step (for moms with young children): Create one calming bedtime ritual. Whether it's reading a story, singing a song, or praying together—create a peaceful moment your child can count on each night.

Goal #19- Survive the Holidays and Make New Traditions

"**S**ee, I am doing a new thing! Now it springs up; do you not perceive it? I am making a way in the wilderness and streams in the wasteland." — Isaiah 43:19 NIV

Holidays can be brutal.

I'm not going to sugarcoat it—they've been some of the most painful days since losing Luke. Especially that first Christmas.

Luke was Mr. Christmas. He absolutely adored everything about the season. By mid-October, Christmas music was already echoing through our home—yes, even before Halloween. We had a lineup of about twenty holiday movies we rewatched every year, and a long list of beloved traditions. It truly was the most magical time of year for our family.

One of my favorite memories is from our last Christmas together in 2019. On Christmas Eve, after the kids went to bed, we would prep for Christmas morning magic. That year, Luke helped me assemble Hayley's bike... then decided to test it out. Picture a 42-year-old leg amputee joyfully pedaling a girl's bike down the street. I'm so glad I grabbed my phone and caught that moment on video. My kids and I still cherish it.

Another unforgettable moment was when Luke put together our then-12-year-old son Payton's Asteroids arcade machine. He was so proud. We captured a video of him grinning like a little kid, playing it himself. These are the memories we hold close—ones that make us smile through the tears.

But with great love comes great loss. And those joyful years made our first Christmas without him even more gut-wrenching.

Luke died in May, so our first holiday without him was Father's Day. It was devastating. We made cards and visited his grave. My boys stayed in the car while Hayley and I sat graveside and cried. We later attended a Father's Day gathering for my dad and brothers, but it was nearly unbearable.

The Fourth of July came next, another rough day since Luke loved fireworks. But nothing hit as hard as our anniversary on August 22nd. He passed away just 3 months shy of what would have been our 17th wedding anniversary. That day, I visited Luke's grave while the kids were at their grandparents. I watched our wedding video and cried alone into my pillow.

Anniversaries are especially painful because no one else really "celebrates" that day except you. It's personal. It's sacred. Even now, after being remarried for two years to Joel (a story for another book), I still mourn on August 22nd. I wonder how we'd celebrate—especially last year, our 20th anniversary. I imagine we would have taken a once-in-a-lifetime trip somewhere beautiful.

That first fall without Luke was rough. Halloween, in particular, was my breaking point.

We'd always gone to the pumpkin patch together. But that year, the hole where Luke should've been was so large and deep, it swallowed any joy. The kids fought. I cried the whole drive home. That was the moment I realized: something had to change.

Trying to recreate holidays exactly as they used to be only magnified his absence. I needed to blend the old with the new—honor what was, while creating what could be.

Thanksgiving was our first major shift. I took the kids to Great Wolf Lodge instead of attending the traditional family meal. My parents came too, and we had pizza instead of turkey. It wasn't perfect—I still cried seeing other families—but it gave us space to breathe and grieve differently.

By Christmas, I had a plan: mix old traditions with new ones.

We went to a different tree farm that year. Luke had always been the one to cut down the tree, and I couldn't handle going back to our usual place without him. So we created a new memory. My brother helped my boys cut down the tree. And you know what? It was a good day. Grief was still there, but less intense. That's what I want to encourage you to do: change something. It helps.

At the same time, we kept traditions like cinnamon rolls (specifically Cinnabon!) on Christmas morning. But we added something new: sharing a favorite memory of Luke before opening gifts. It's become a cherished moment of remembrance in our home.

Another tradition we've adapted is placing the star on top of the tree. That was always Luke's job. Now, each of our kids takes turns doing "Daddy's job." They love when it's their turn. I hope it's something they continue as adults.

We also add ornaments each year—some in Luke's memory, and some that represent new milestones or joyful moments.

Valentine's Day is hard. Luke used to joke it was a made-up Hallmark holiday—but he still took me out every year. Before I remarried, I made fun plans with friends. One year, we hosted a "Galantine's Day," and it was genuinely fun. I also avoided social media on that day—it helped not seeing couple posts all day long.

On Luke's birthday we make his favorite cherry chip cake and go to Red Robin—his favorite restaurant. I share pictures and messages on social media to honor him.

Every year on Luke's death anniversary, the kids and I go to his favorite restaurant—Red Robin—and we each share something from the past year that we are proud of that we would have wanted to tell him. It's our way of honoring him and staying connected to his memory.

That first year, I also cooked and recreated the last meal I made for Luke—grilled cheese sandwiches—and we released balloon messages. I created a memorial video and decided that day to take off my wedding ring. It was a deeply personal moment of letting go and choosing to move forward.In the years since, we continue to visit his grave and honor him in ways that feel right for us. Joel supports this time, giving me space and even gifting flowers to place on Luke's grave.

The firsts are the hardest. But with time, healing, and intentional effort, the holidays become more manageable. Not pain-free—but manageable. Give yourself permission to change what you need. Keep what matters. Let go of what hurts. And build new traditions rooted in love, memory, and hope. You've got this, my friend. Truly, you do.

PS- I would love to email and pray for you on these difficult days, be sure to scan the QR code in the back of the book so I can do this for you!

Widow Reflections

1. Which holiday or special occasion has been the most challenging for you since your loss, and why?

2. What traditions from your past have brought you comfort, and which ones have been difficult to continue?

3. Think about a time when you changed something about a holiday to make it more bearable. What worked well, and what might you do differently next time to continue finding healing in these moments?

Widow Action Steps

*Choose one tradition that brings pain and reimagine it in a new way this year—whether it's the place, the meal, or the company.

*Create a meaningful way to honor your spouse during the holidays (a memory jar, a shared story, or a special ornament).

*Make a plan for your most difficult date (anniversary, birthday, or death anniversary) so that you aren't caught off guard—include people, space, or comfort items that support your heart.

Goal #20— Consider Counseling or Other Grief Programs

"The Lord is close to the brokenhearted and saves those who are crushed in spirit." Psalm 34:18 NIV

If you broke your arm but never had it set, what would happen? It wouldn't heal properly—it would remain damaged, crooked, and likely painful.

Now picture getting a flat tire. Instead of fixing it, you just stare at it for days, hoping it will magically inflate. A week from now? Still flat. A year from now? Still flat.

That's what grief can look like when we leave it untouched. And that's why one of the biggest myths we need to stop believing is this: "Time heals."

I used to believe it myself. I even told others the same thing. But I learned the truth: it wasn't time that was healing me—it was what I was doing with that time. If I had waited and done nothing, I would've stayed stuck, just like that flat tire. I would've remained broken in ways no amount of wishing could fix.

So how do we actually heal? We make our healing a priority.

I've met so many widows who are in the exact same place emotionally five or ten years after their spouse's death. At first, I didn't understand it. But the more I studied grief and walked through it myself, the clearer it became. Some people never do the work—or they don't access the right tools.

And as strange as it sounds, some grow attached to their grief. It becomes their identity. Their pain becomes their story.

But if you're reading this book, I know that's not you. You want joy to return. You want to feel whole again. You want to live, not just survive.

Healing comes one step at a time. One day at a time. One book at a time. One program at a time.

Reading books like this—and others—will help you gain understanding and equip you with tools to move forward. Here are a few that I found particularly valuable:

- The *Grief Recovery Handbook* by John W. James and Russell Friedman

- *It's OK That You're Not OK: Meeting Grief and Loss in a Culture That Doesn't Understand* by Megan Devine

- *The Positive Widow: The Four Simple Ways to HOPE and Healing After Loss* by Christina Napoleon

I also highly recommend The Grief Recovery Method Program. Even after two years of grief work, this program helped me uncover areas I didn't know were still unhealed. It walks you through every loss you've experienced, with a deep focus on your most significant loss—likely your spouse. Whether in a group or one-on-one, in person or via Zoom, it provides a safe and guided path to emotional recovery.

If you're curious, visit www.thegriefrecoverymethod.com to find a certified specialist or group in your area.

Now let me ask you: How important is your healing to you? Do you want to be in the same place a year from now?

When I was a brand-new widow—or "baby widow," as I like to say—I was desperate to feel better. I dove into every resource I could find: books, groups, counseling, retreats. And guess what?

It worked. Slowly. Quietly. Sometimes so subtly that I didn't even notice it until I looked back. But healing happened. And it can happen for you too.

I've been seeing my counselor for over fifteen years. She walked with me through Luke's cancer journey and his passing, and I still meet with her at least once a month. Therapy has been one of the most important investments I've made in myself.

Some people think counseling is only for when you're "really struggling." But I believe it's an act of strength. A way of saying, "I'm worth healing." Counselors are professional secret-keepers with the outside perspective we often need. And if cost is a barrier, look into nonprofits or churches that offer sliding scales. Many insurance plans also cover therapy.

You're here because you want a better future. Maybe you picked up this book out of desperation, or maybe someone gave it to you. Whatever brought you here, I know one thing: You don't want to stay in this same place forever.

You owe it to yourself—and your future—to take grief recovery seriously. Find a counselor. Join a program. Do the work. Look up resources. Talk to someone. Take one small, bold step toward healing today.

There's no way around grief. You can't go over it or under it. The only way is through. But the good news? Others have gone before you—and you don't have to walk alone.

Don't let time, pride, or money stop you from healing. Don't let silence win.

This is your lifeline: Get help. You're not broken. You're brave. You're not fragile. You're strong. You were never meant to do this alone.

Widow Reflections

1. How have I been approaching my grief recovery? Am I waiting for time to heal me, or am I actively seeking the right tools and support?

2. What steps can I take today to prioritize my healing?

3. Whether it's reaching out for counseling or committing to a grief support group, what is one thing I can do today to move forward?

Widow Action Steps

*Research and contact one counseling service or grief recovery program. Look into local or virtual options, such as The Grief Recovery Method, church-based grief groups, or a licensed counselor. Make one phone call or send one email this week.

*Make a list of books, podcasts, or courses focused on grief healing. Commit to reading or listening to at least one resource this month that will add a new tool to your healing toolkit.

*Set a "healing appointment" with yourself. Whether it's journaling, praying, or simply reflecting, set aside 30 minutes this week to ask yourself: How am I really doing? Use this time to take one intentional step forward.

Goal #21– Understand How Much God Loves and Defends Widows

"**A** *father to the fatherless, a defender of widows, is God in his holy dwelling.*" Psalm 68:5 NIV

You may feel forgotten—but you are not. You may feel exposed—but you are fiercely protected. As a widow, you are not just noticed by God—you are defended by Him.

From cover to cover, the Bible makes it clear: widows hold a sacred place in God's heart. He doesn't just comfort us—He fights for us.

Do you have any idea how much God loves you? Do you know that widows hold a special place in His heart? Guess how many times widows are mentioned in the Bible? The word widow has been mentioned 103 times in the New International Version (NIV) Bible.

I remember the first time I heard Psalm 68:5 after I was widowed. I'm sure I had heard it many times throughout my life, but it didn't mean much to me. When I read it after Luke died, it took on an entirely different meaning. God is a defender of widows and a father to the fatherless. That was me and my kids! How could there be a verse so specific to my children and me? In my time as a widow, I have seen this verse ring true over and over.

What does it mean to be defended? It means God watches out for us. He is by our side, helping us through all of our new challenges as widows. That doesn't mean we won't have any trials or trouble, but it's a promise that He will defend us as we go through them.

I picture God as a giant warrior walking in front of me, His sword destroying the things meant to destroy me. I walk behind Him as He shows me where to step. Many times He catches me right before I fall into a deep, dark pit that I didn't see coming. He lovingly picks up my children and meets their hearts in only the way a Father can. He places all three of them on His broad shoulders as I follow behind. He guides us up the treacherous mountains of deep grief. He reaches up to catch the tears of my children and gently holds my hand so that I will not fall. He guides us down into the grassy valley of peace, and He gives us a resting spot in the cool shade next to a peaceful babbling brook and lets us rest awhile.

Even before Luke's death, I felt this way too. I was in the parking lot of Walmart when Luke's oncologist called to tell me that there was nothing else to be done to fight his cancer.

"How much time do you think he has left?" My voice quivered as I didn't really want to hear the answer.

"Six to nine months," his emotionless voice responded.

I don't remember what I said next, or hanging up the phone, or really much of anything at all. In a daze, I walked into Walmart, still needing to complete the task I came for. I remember feeling like I was walking in slow motion and all those around me were walking quickly, in a blur.

I thought, "They have no idea what I am going through. The laughing boy and the hurried mom have no idea that I was just told the life expectancy of my husband."

Suddenly the words I had memorized as a child came rushing into my mind: "Though I walk through the valley of the shadow of death, I will fear no evil." Psalm 23:4 KJV

I repeated these 13 small but powerful words over and over as I wandered aimlessly down the aisles. Walking through the valley of the shadow of death was the hardest thing I ever had to do.

You know this same pain, my friend. You understand firsthand what it means to walk through the valley of the shadow of death. It's a shadow darker than any other shadow I know. But what I have found is that when I am in the darkest place, God's love shines the brightest. His light is always there—I'm just more aware of it when I am in complete darkness.

How do you explain complete darkness? Well, I believe the technical term is the absence of light. But what does it feel like? Death. Mourning. Intense pain. Agony. Suffering. Sadness. These words remind me of the darkest moment there ever was: the moment Jesus died. The moment He died a cruel, painful, agonizing death. The day He died for me. The day He died for you.

Jesus understands firsthand what suffering is. He's not just some God up in heaven watching from afar. He has lived the pain we feel. That is so comforting to me—to know that He really gets it.

Just in case you don't know the end of the story—Jesus didn't stay in that place. He rose again! Hallelujah! He is the reason we can have eternal life.

"For God so loved the world that he gave his one and only Son, that whoever believes in him shall not perish but have eternal life." — John 3:16 NIV

This life is not the end of the story. When you've lost someone you love—especially a spouse—this part of the verse becomes even more precious. Eternal life means that death doesn't get the final say. God promises hope beyond this moment and reunion beyond the grave.

If you haven't already invited Jesus into your life to forgive you of your sins and be the Lord of your life, I invite you to do it now.

These verses are reminders of how deeply God sees, defends, and provides for His widows:

- Psalm 68:5 (NIV) – "A *father to the fatherless, a defender of widows, is God in his holy dwelling.*"

- Psalm 146:9 (NIV) – "*The Lord watches over the foreigner and sustains the fatherless and the widow, but he frustrates the ways of the wicked.*"

- Deuteronomy 10:18 (NIV) – "*He defends the cause of the fatherless and the widow, and loves the foreigner residing among you, giving them food and clothing.*"

- 1 Kings 17:14-16 (NIV) – God provides for the widow of Zarephath: "*The jar of flour will not be used up and the jug of oil will not run dry...*"

- Luke 7:12-15 (NIV) – Jesus raises a widow's son and says, "Don't cry." His heart goes out to her.

- Luke 21:2-3 (NIV) – Jesus honors the widow's offering: "*This poor widow has put in more than all the others.*"

- James 1:27 (NIV) – "*Religion that God our Father accepts as pure and faultless is this: to look after orphans and widows in their distress...*"

- Isaiah 1:17 (NIV) – "*Learn to do right; seek justice. Defend the oppressed. Take up the cause of the fatherless; plead the case of the widow.*"

- Jeremiah 7:6 (NIV) – "*Do not oppress the foreigner, the fatherless or the widow...*"

- Malachi 3:5 (NIV) – "*So I will come to put you on trial... against those who defraud laborers, who oppress the widows and the fatherless...*"

So, when the days feel unbearably heavy and the nights stretch long and lonely, remember this: you are not invisible to God. You are seen. You are cherished. And you are fiercely defended. You are not just part of a sad story—your life is part of His redemption story. God hasn't abandoned you; in fact, He draws especially near to widows. He is your Provider, your Protector, your steady place when the world has shifted beneath you.

You are not walking this road alone. The Defender of widows goes before you, stands beside you, and will never stop fighting for your heart. Let that truth root deep into your soul—you are loved, covered, and held by the God who never lets go.

Widow Reflections

1, How have you experienced God defending or providing for you in your widow journey?

2. Which Bible verse from this chapter spoke most deeply to your heart—and why?

3. What would it look like this week to trust God as your Defender in one specific area of your life?

Widow Action Steps

*Write a Letter to God as Your Defender- Pour out your heart in a letter to God, thanking Him for the ways He has protected you and asking Him to continue guiding and defending you and your family.

*Choose One "Widow Verse" to Memorize and Meditate On- Pick one of the scriptures listed in this chapter that speaks to your soul. Write it on a notecard, save it as your phone background, or post it on your bathroom mirror.

*Create a "God's Provision" Journal Entry- List at least five specific ways God has provided for or defended you since your spouse's death—financially, emotionally, spiritually, or through others

Goal #22 – Know That It's Okay to Be Angry

"The Lord is close to the brokenhearted and saves those who are crushed in spirit." –Psalm 34:18 NIV

Somewhere along the way, many of us we're taught that we're not supposed to be angry—especially not at God. But let me tell you the truth: I've had moments where I was downright furious with Him.

I was just 24 years old, newly married, and overflowing with joy, when our world came crashing down with Luke's cancer diagnosis. I remember being mad—no, livid. Angry at the unfairness. Angry at the word cancer. Angry that while my friends were busy planning babies, I was wondering if my husband would live. (If you want to know more about that season of my life, I share our story in my book *Cancer Can't Crush Us – A Newlywed's Journey Through Faith, Love & Cancer*.)[1]

After we found out Luke's diagnosis, I remember walking into our bedroom, closing the curtains, and collapsing on the bed in a mess of tears and screams. "Why us, God?" I cried. I was 24! Newlywed! I didn't sign up for this. I didn't sign up for 16.5 years

---

1. Michelle Bader, Cancer Can't Crush Us: A Newlywed's Journey Through Faith, Love & Cancer (Vancouver, WA: Michelle Bader, 2020).

of hospitals, diagnoses, complications, and a husband whose body was constantly under attack.

There were seasons when it felt like the anger would swallow me whole. I had three kids under four, and Luke was so sick he couldn't help. Why him? Why us? The questions came in waves, and so did the anger.

And then came the grief. After Luke died, the anger returned in a brand-new, raw way. I was 41 years old—a widow. A solo parent to three teenagers. Remember the walks I told you about with Jesus? Some of those included me yelling at the top of my lungs:

"Why me, God? Why did you choose me for this? You've got the wrong girl—I can't do this!"

Tears streaming, fists clenched, heart shattered. And yet, every single time I let it out, I found that God could take it. He didn't shame me or turn away. He met me there. In the yelling, in the breakdown, in the sobbing heap on the floor—He was there. And after the storm, His peace would wash over me like a gentle river, soothing my soul in ways words can't fully explain.

If you're angry today—angry that you're widowed, that your life looks nothing like what you planned—it's okay. If you need to yell at God, He can handle it. He sees through your fury to your hurting, broken heart.

And here's what I've learned: when we're honest with God, that's when the healing begins. He doesn't want us to pretend. He wants a relationship with us. Relationships are built through honesty, not masks. You can come to Him with every messy, real emotion.

Just remember: anger is okay to visit, but not to live in. I've seen widows stay parked in their anger, and it only delays the healing. It becomes like a poison that pushes peace out of our hearts. My recommendation is: feel it, face it, and then release it.

Sometimes, anger needs a physical outlet. Maybe you've heard of rage rooms—places where you can smash things like TVs or toilets with a sledgehammer. I haven't tried one (yet!), but it sounds kind of amazing. For me, my outlet has always been running or pounding my punching bag. Nothing like turning up some good ol' angry 90s music—hello Nirvana—and running out every bit of rage until I'm breathless and free.

Whether it's a physical release or a walk-and-yell session with Jesus, give yourself permission to let it out. And not just once. Anger tends to return, especially as new hurts or injustices occur. When it rises again, go back through the process: feel it, talk to God about it, and let it go.

Healing doesn't mean you'll never feel anger again—it just means you won't stay stuck in it. Let God meet you there and carry you through to the other side.

Anger is not a sin—it's a signal. A sign that something deeply painful has happened. And God doesn't ask us to clean up our hearts before coming to Him. He invites us to bring our raw, unfiltered hearts straight to His feet.

Remember, God can handle your honesty. He already knows your thoughts, so you might as well share them. And when you do, you open the door to His peace: a peace that will surprise you, hold you, and carry you when you feel like you can't go on.

You, my friend, are not alone in your anger. You are seen, heard, and deeply loved—even in your fiercest storms.

Widow Reflections

1. What are sone of the moments when you've felt anger during your grief journey? How did you respond?

2. Have you been honest with God about your anger? If not, what's holding you back?

3. What physical or creative outlets could help you release your anger in a healthy way?

Widow Action Steps

*Write a letter to God expressing your anger—uncensored and unfiltered.

*Choose a physical outlet to release your emotions. It could be a walk, a workout, painting, or even punching a pillow. Find what works for you.

*Set a time this week to talk honestly with God about your anger. No filter. Just real, raw connection. Let that conversation be a step toward healing.

Goal #23– Know That Finding Love Again Is Okay

"**Y**ou have turned for me my mourning into dancing; you have loosed my sackcloth and clothed me with gladness." Psalms 30:11 ESV

If you are not ready to even think about this subject, that's okay. You can return to it if you're ever ready—or just read it to hear my thoughts. I remember the first time someone said to me, "You are young; you'll find someone else." At that moment, I was so deep in grief that the idea of dating again felt like cheating. It made me physically sick. If that's how you're feeling right now, you are not alone—and you're not ready. And that's okay.

There is no right or wrong timeline for when it's okay to date again. It is up to you. We all have different journeys.

From working with widows and through my personal experience, I've noticed that those of us who experienced anticipatory grief—grieving before our spouse passed due to a prolonged illness—sometimes feel ready to date sooner. Not always, but sometimes. When Luke was sick, a friend explained anticipatory grief to me like this: It's like standing on a train track. You can see the train coming, so you are bracing for impact as you know the end is near.

For the first several months after Luke died, dating sounded awful. Then one morning, I woke up and thought, "Hmm, it might be fun to start talking to men again." And that's how it started. Just a small thought that led to a few online conversations.

Friends, if you haven't dated in the last decade or two, it's a whole new world. When Luke and I were dating, texting wasn't even a thing—now we have full-on social media. You can learn just about everything about someone's life online.

In one of my widow groups, I heard about Facebook Dating. I had never even known it existed. It was so easy. One click, and I had a profile. Instantly, my phone exploded with notifications. I had no idea that would happen! A sea of men wanted to talk to me.

I made a mistake right away: I shared that I was widowed, and I learned that this can make you a target for scams. Even though I selected that I only wanted to talk to Christians, all kinds of men came out of the woodwork. Some who claimed to be Christians moved to inappropriate conversations immediately. One guy wanted to meet me the first day we chatted. I was not ready—and I never went out with him.

I remember the first time I was alone with a man—a friend I'd known since I was a teen. We went for a walk, and I felt like I was cheating on Luke. My brain struggled to comprehend that I was allowed to be with someone else. If you feel these conflicting feelings too, you are not alone.

My post-Luke relationship journey was rocky, to say the least. But eventually, it led me to Joel—who is now my husband.

Joel and I went to college together over twenty years ago. I always thought of him as the "cute guy with the Brazilian accent," but that was it. We both married and had children. One day, while scrolling Facebook, I saw his name as a suggested friend. I hadn't thought of him in years, but now, as a newly single woman, I clicked on his profile.

That was July 2021. We were married on March 18, 2023.

We video chatted for a few months, then started a long-distance relationship. I was in Washington, and he was in Louisiana. He had family in my area, so after talking for a few months he came out to meet me and visit his family. He told me he loved me the first time we met. I also knew and told him that I loved him too. We found ways to see each other once a month. I knew quickly that he was what I wanted.

I used to say I only wanted to date a widower. But I remained open to whatever plan God had for me. Joel is divorced, and while those experiences are different, it's not about how their past relationship ended—it's about the qualities and the characteristics of the person with whom you are willing to have a relationship. Joel has always respected my grief. He gives me space on grief days, brings flowers to Luke's grave, and is okay with us having Luke's photos in our home. He even asks questions about Luke.

If you're dating someone who is jealous of your late spouse—run. If they don't like you talking about him, posting about him, or having pictures—please leave that situation immediately!

Dating in your 40s is very different than in your 20s. Going into the process with that understanding helps. There's no right way to find your next great love. Some people use apps, get set up by friends, or meet someone organically.

Early on in my dating journey, I was crying to my best friend after a particularly hard end of a relationship. "Where will I ever find someone at my age?" She replied, "Let God write your love story." That changed everything.

In the period of waiting, focus on becoming whole. Focus on healing. Prepare your heart for what's to come. I've heard so many stories of God bringing couples together in miraculous ways. If you desire love again, trust that He has a story for you too—but in His perfect timing.

One of the biggest myths about dating after loss is that another love will cancel out your love for your late spouse. That's not true. If you have kids, think about when you had your second child. Did loving your second child take love away from the first? No. Your heart simply expanded. That's how it is with finding love again.

I will forever love Luke. And I deeply love Joel.

Some people think that how long you wait to date equals how much you loved your spouse. False. People online (usually not widowed) often share opinions that are unhelpful and uninformed. Don't fall into the trap of forcing yourself to wait just to "prove" how much you cared.

You will likely feel grief while dating. I did. And still do. After relationships ended, I felt the sting even more—because if I hadn't been widowed, I wouldn't be dating. I still grieve on the anniversary of my wedding to Luke. That day was uniquely ours. Even being happily married again, I still wake up wondering what it would be like if Luke were alive.

I miss the completeness of a family where both parents love our kids equally. Joel is wonderful and loves them deeply. But I still miss that bond Luke and I shared over our children.

A few days before marrying Joel, I visited Luke's grave. I cried and told him I was getting married again, but I would always love him. Joel and I even acknowledged Luke in our wedding.

Here's what I shared at our ceremony:

Thank you so much for coming here to celebrate this joyous day with us. We understand that today will be filled with many emotions, some of them conflicting. We want you to know that whatever you are feeling is okay.

For we would not be here today if both of our families had not experienced countless tears and years of grief. We ask that if you come here today with lots of happiness and excitement, take a deep breath and realize that while today is joyful and beautiful, for some, it's also a reminder of what isn't anymore.

We ask that you pray for those deeply affected by that pain.

Neither Joel nor I—or our kids—got here without experiencing bro-kenness: the loss of a husband and dad, and the death of a marriage and family unit.

If you came into this wedding with sadness, know that we hold that too. We pray that you can see the beauty in the uniting of families and feel joy today. In our lives, both separately and together, we've seen God turn mourning into dancing and bring beauty from ashes. It is okay to feel both happiness and sadness. One does not cancel the other. What we feel, we heal.

Over two years ago, I felt God promise me He would redeem and restore what I had lost and bring back the joy of my youth. And here we are today—His promise fulfilled in a way I never imagined. God is the ultimate healer and restorer of hearts, and we pray you see and feel that today.

We wanted our guests to know—whatever they were feeling, it was valid. Joy and sorrow can live side by side.

It was the happiest day of my life, yet there was sadness. My kids experienced grief watching me marry someone who wasn't their dad.

Dating can feel overwhelming. Just take it one moment at a time. One date doesn't mean you'll marry that person. Enjoy the journey. The crazy dates will give you great stories! (Don't even get me started on the guy whose profile photo had a shirt that said "I Love Hot Moms." Naturally, I was a good fit. LOL!)

If you're considering dating, pray for your future partner. Ask God to protect you from the wrong ones. And don't be surprised if strange things start happening—remember, rejection can be God's protection. Let your story unfold at your own pace, in your own way with God's leading. You are not alone.

Widow Reflections

1. How do you feel about the idea of dating or finding love again after loss? What emotions—hope, fear, guilt—rise up when you think about this possibility?

2. Are there specific values or boundaries that are important to you in a new relationship?

3. How can you honor the memory of your late spouse while also making space in your heart for a new chapter?

Widow Action Steps

*Write a letter to your future partner, even if you haven't met them yet. Share your hopes, values, and what kind of love you're praying for.

*Make a list of red flags in relationships to help you navigate wisely when you begin dating.

*Spend time in prayer asking God to heal your heart and guide your steps if and when you're ready to open your heart to love again.

Goal #24– Give Yourself Permission to Remember Honestly–Even the Hard Parts

"**B**ut I will restore you to health and heal your wounds," declares the Lord." Jeremiah 30:17 NIV

No one told me grief would ask me to rewrite my memories—but it did. If I could go back and whisper something to my newly widowed self, it would be this: It's okay to remember it all—the good, the bad, and everything in between.

Let's be honest. When someone dies, we tend to put their memory on a pedestal. I remember hearing that old phrase growing up: "Don't speak ill of the dead." It sounded noble, respectful... even spiritual. But here's what I've come to learn: that phrase, while well-intentioned, can be incredibly damaging to someone who's grieving.

When Luke died, I didn't say a single negative word about him for months. Not one. It wasn't until I was sitting in my counselor's office that I was finally given permission to speak the full truth. She gently said, "Even though Luke died, the facts are still the facts. Those things happened." And wow—those words unlocked something in me.

Now, if you had the perfect marriage and your spouse could do no wrong, maybe you'll skip this chapter. But let's be real, friends: no one had a perfect marriage. We're imperfect people doing the best we can in a broken world. Our relationships were real and messy, full of beautiful highs and difficult lows.

You're not dishonoring your spouse by acknowledging the whole story. You're being honest. And honesty is where healing begins.

But let me be clear—I'm not saying you should blast the hard parts on social media or bring them up in the wrong setting. Honesty doesn't mean publicizing pain. It means giving your heart the gift of being heard in the right space—with someone who sees you, hears you, and won't rush your healing. That could be a licensed therapist, a counselor, or your very best friend. Someone who will hold space for your story without judgment.

Over the years, I've worked with so many widows carrying unresolved pain—wounds that never had the chance to heal because death came too soon. And when we don't deal with that pain, it doesn't just disappear. It lingers. It festers. It shows up in ways we don't always recognize.

When we pretend our spouse was perfect and only tell the highlight reel, we lose part of the truth. And the truth, as hard as it may be, is where freedom lives.

I've said this a million times on my podcast *Widowed 2 Soon*, and I'll say it again here: What we feel, God can heal.

If you keep those hard memories buried deep, locked behind fear or guilt, you're not giving God the chance to bring His healing light into those places. You're not giving yourself the chance to heal fully.

Here's the beautiful and unexpected truth I've found: when we process the hard stuff, the good memories begin to rise to the surface again. It's like our hearts finally have space to breathe.

There's even science to back this up. Therapies like EMDR (Eye Movement Desensitization and Reprocessing) and cognitive processing therapy show that when trauma is left unprocessed, it clutters the brain. It keeps us stuck in survival mode. But once we bring those memories into the light and integrate them, the brain begins to calm. It makes room for joy again. For laughter. For love.

This principle is known as memory reconsolidation—and I've lived it. I've seen it in the lives of countless others walking this grief journey too. Once we allow ourselves to go there—to revisit those dark corners—we start to rediscover things we thought were gone forever. Little moments. Inside jokes. That contagious laugh. The way they looked at you when they didn't know you were watching.

I'm not saying it's easy—because it's not. Healing takes work. But here's the beautiful part: healing brings healing. And in the process, it often uncovers beauty we didn't even realize we had lost. So, friend, please hear my heart: I'm not asking you to dwell on the pain. I'm asking you to face the truth.

The highest highs
The lowest lows.
The real marriage.
The full story.
Because you deserve to be free.

Early in my grief, I always presented Luke in the most perfect light—especially to our kids. But as they've grown, they've started asking more questions about some of the harder memories they hold. And I've had the opportunity to share with them honestly. To validate their experiences. To grieve with them. To grow with them.

You know your children. You know what's appropriate to share. And some things are meant only for your therapist or your most trusted friend. But I want to give you permission today: you're allowed to remember the hard parts.

This is something I rarely see talked about in the grief community. I get it—there's a time and place for everything. But I believe this step is a vital part of healing.

Because where there is truth, there is light. And where there is light, there is freedom.

And friend—freedom is a gift God longs for you to have.

Widow Reflections

1. What are some memories—good or hard—that you've felt hesitant to acknowledge or speak out loud?

2. Have you ever felt guilt about thinking negatively of your spouse after their passing? How can you reframe that to embrace both truth and grace?

3. Who is someone safe you can talk to about the full picture of your marriage—a person who can help you process without judgment?

Widow Action Steps

*Take a few quiet moments to reflect on one difficult memory you've been hesitant to revisit. Write it down in your journal. Bringing it into the light is the first step toward healing.

*Choose a person—a therapist, grief counselor, or trusted confidant—with whom you can share both the beautiful and the hard parts of your story. Honesty in a safe space creates room for true healing.

*In prayer or reflection, intentionally invite God into the full picture of your marriage and loss. Ask Him to help you process the pain, restore the broken pieces, and help you hold space for truth, grace, and freedom.

Goal #25– Gently Guide Others in How to Support You

"The tongue has the power of life and death, and those who love it will eat its fruit." Proverbs 18:21 NIV

Has anyone ever said something to you about your grief that made you cringe or think, "Did they really say that to me?!" I am sure we all have experienced this, and that is why I created this chapter. I have worked with countless people who have experienced grief, and through my own experiences and all of theirs, I have pretty much heard it all! However, I believe that most people who say unhelpful things to us do mean well. I have learned to listen to their hearts and not their words.

Please share this chapter with the people you love. Many well-meaning individuals inadvertently say the wrong thing because they focus on what might be intellectually true rather than what is emotionally helpful—a concept I learned through The Grief Recovery Handbook[1]. For instance, the saying "They are in a better place" may be intellectually true, but it's not emotionally helpful. The key is to listen actively.

---

1. The Grief Recovery Handbook: The Action Program for Moving Beyond Death, Divorce, and Other Losses (New York: HarperCollins, 2009).

Use this QR code to get the PDF of the content below to send to your friends and family.

A Summary of Unhelpful Comments That Should Not Be Said to Those Grieving:

- "I know how you feel; my _____ died." No, you don't. Even if you are also widowed, you don't know our unique individual story or how I feel. This kind of comparison can be hurtful and dismissive of the griever's unique experience.

- "How did they die?" This is usually asked out of pure curiosity. If they want to share, they will; but please don't make anyone uncomfortable by asking this question.

- "I know how you feel. I'm divorced." Don't even get me started on this one. Any comparison of grief is inappropriate. But the attempt to compare a situation where no one's life has ended to that of one whose spouse has died is excruciatingly hurtful and wildly inappropriate! Just don't do it.

- "God just needed another angel." First, according to the Bible, we don't become angels when we die. Second, God does not need anything. Enough said.

- "At least you had this many years together; at least you did this or that."If it has the words "at least" in it, don't say it. It belittles what we did have and is not helpful.

- "You are young; you will find someone else." While this may be true, it is not helpful at all. I remember shortly after Luke died when someone said this to me, and it made me sick to my stomach. Yes, it was true, and I eventually married again, but it didn't help me at that moment.

- "God won't give you more than you can handle." THIS! I have always considered myself strong, but this statement was not helpful. First of all, there is no verse in the Bible about this concept, despite what many people think. They confuse it with verses that talk about God never letting you be tempted beyond what you can handle (1 Corinthians 10:13 (NIV)), and secondly, it just doesn't help the widow feel any better.

- "You should stay busy." This is a HUGE grief myth! Beyond being unhelpful, this comment can actually be detrimental to one grieving the loss of a spouse. When you tell them to stay busy, you tell them not to feel. The only way through grief is to feel it. So, when this statement is said, it is encouraging the widow to suppress the pain. The problem is that the pain will resurface if not properly addressed. Please don't say this to anyone grieving!

- "I can't imagine what you are going through." This is not even true. We all have imaginations. If the person telling us wanted to, they could close their eyes and imagine to the best of their ability what it would feel like to lose a spouse. It also doesn't come across as very kind or caring. Let's stop doing this.

- "They wouldn't want you to be sad." This tells the griever that they shouldn't be acting the way they are. It gives the message that there is a right or wrong way to grieve.

- "Time heals." This is another huge grief myth! Through Grief Recovery, I learned the truth about why this myth is false. It is not just the time passing that does the healing; it is what you do with the time. Imagine I had a flat tire on my car. I parked it in my garage and said, "I'll just give it time, and it will heal." We all know how unrealistic that is, right? If we were to get air and put it in the tire, then it could be usable again. So it is about what you do with the time, not how much time has passed. Also, in my personal experience and in my work with hundreds of widows, I have discovered those who experienced anticipatory grief and knew their loved one was dying often start their healing much quicker than those who had no warning. This makes sense because they have spent additional time grieving.

- "At least they're no longer suffering." Yes, it's true, and I know that comment is meant to be helpful and comforting. However, it minimizes a widow's profound loss and sorrow.

- "I didn't reach out because I didn't know what to say." This statement conveys that the person is prioritizing their feelings over those of the one grieving. We prefer that you say, "Just listen; you don't have to know what to say."

- "At least you have your kids at home to keep you company." This may be true, but caring for grieving children while you are grieving yourself is exhausting. Maybe sometimes they wish their kids had been older and had their parents all their growing-up years.

- "At least you don't have kids at home; that would be so much harder." This could also be true but not helpful—and it means you are completely alone.

- "Let me know if you ever need anything." The griever usually has no idea what they need and probably won't have the energy, the organization skills, or the courage to ask you when they think of something.

What You Can Say and Do to Help a Widow/Widower:
There are so many helpful things that you can say and do, so let's focus on the positive and help improve a griever's life.

- Be assured that often the most powerful support is your presence. Let the griever know you're there for them, and then simply listen.

- "It's okay to feel how you are feeling right now." This is so helpful because it gives the griever permission to be any way they want. If they want to laugh, they can laugh. If they want to cry, they can cry. Create a judgment-free space.

- "Your love for them was so evident. I am here if you want to share a story about them." They may or may not want to do this. I have always found it healing to share stories about Luke. You can also share your own stories about your loved ones if you have them.

- "Can I help you with _____?" (laundry, meals, taking kids, etc.) Be very specific and fill in the blanks with tasks such as laundry, meals, transporting the kids, etc. I loved it when people told me specific things they could do so I didn't have to figure it out alone.

- "I don't know how you feel, but you can share how you are feeling." This way, you are not invalidating their feelings, and they have the freedom to share.

- "Grief has no timeline; take all the time you need." This is a great way to relieve them of the pressure of thinking they should be at a specific point, depending on the timeline.

- "You don't have to go through this alone; I am here for you." This is a powerful statement—BUT only say this if you can and will continue to show up long after the celebration of life has ended.

One of the most challenging times in a widow's life is after the celebration of life—when the cards and meals stop coming. For months, I felt supported and loved. My mind was occupied with planning Luke's celebration of life. But when it was all over and my last guest left, I was alone again—face-to-face with the emptiness of Luke being gone.

The loneliness came flooding in, and I really needed my friends. If you love and support a widow/widower, this is go-time. Everyone is there initially, but it takes special people who love us to continue showing up when the rest of the world has forgotten. Be there for them during that time. Go further and be there for them on all the hard anniversary dates. Please put the date their spouse died in your calendar and set an alarm to remind you every year.

The date that Luke died—May 23rd—is one of my most challenging days. To me and my kids, it's the day our world stopped, but to most people, it's just another day on the calendar. Almost five years later, hardly anyone remembers, but to those few beautiful souls who continue to reach out to me every year (shout out to my mom, Melissa Sutton, and Deborah Johnston), it means more to me than I can adequately express. So please, keep a record of this date, and reach out with love and support every year. While you're at it, ask them about their wedding anniversary date and the birthday of their loved one. They will be so touched and blessed if you remember to reach out to them on all of these days.

Dear sweet friend or family member of a widow/widower, thank you for loving them enough to read this list. Being widowed is a lonely journey, and having a team of people in our corner can make all the difference in the world. Your presence, your care, your willingness to learn—it brings hope to someone who may not feel it right now. You are part of the healing. You are part of the light. And that makes you a true gift.

Widow Reflections

1- What is one thing someone said to you after your loss that was unintentionally hurtful?

2- Who in your life has truly shown up for you in your grief journey?

3- If you could kindly educate one person about how to support you better, what would you want them to know?

Widow Action Steps

*Use the downloadable PDF linked in this chapter to gently educate your friends and family. Choose 2–3 people you trust and send it to them this week.

*Add key anniversary dates to a shared calendar. -Identify the most meaningful dates (death anniversary, birthday, wedding anniversary) and ask a few trusted friends to mark them on their calendars with a yearly reminder.

*Make a list of helpful vs. unhelpful comments. Reflect on what words lifted you up and which ones stung. Then, draft your own "do say/don't say" list. You can even turn this into a letter or post to share with your friends and family, guiding them with love.

Goal #26-Know That You Were Chosen

"Y̲ou did not choose me, but I chose you and appointed you so that you might go and bear fruit—fruit that will last." John 15:16 NIV

Have you ever whispered through tears, "Why me?"I have. And for a long time, I believed being chosen for this heartbreak meant I was being punished.But what if being chosen doesn't mean punishment—what if it means you were trusted?

Let me share a moment that forever changed my perspective.

My husband, Luke, died in May of 2020, right in the thick of the COVID-19 pandemic. As if grief wasn't hard enough, the world had shut down. Only ten people were allowed at his graveside service. Community was almost nonexistent when I needed it the most. I felt completely alone in my pain.

Then, out of nowhere, I heard about a grief retreat being held less than an hour from my house. I signed up immediately, made arrangements for my kids, and prayed that this would be the breath of fresh air I so desperately needed. I longed to be around people who truly got it.

The retreat was beautiful—set in the Columbia Gorge with sweeping views of the river. Interestingly, this would later be the same place where we held Luke's Celebration of Life, after my church couldn't accommodate us due to gathering restrictions. The retreat center graciously opened their space.

That first night, the retreat leader explained an activity we'd be doing:

"We have three wooden crosses overlooking the river," she began. "Tonight, I want you to imagine Jesus on that cross. Look into His eyes. Feel His pain. Internalize what He did for you. You'll dip your hands in red paint to represent His blood, place your hands on the cross, and imagine that moment with Him."

I was a little hesitant. It felt unorthodox. But I was willing to try anything if it would help ease the crushing weight I was carrying. I was only two months out from Luke's death, and my heart was completely broken.

As fellow grievers and I made our way outside under a blanket of stars—free from city lights—I could hear soft music playing. People were lined up at the crosses. Then, I heard it. The song we had played at Luke's graveside service: *The Blessing* by Kari Jobe. I hadn't heard it since that day, avoiding it because I knew it would unravel me. But somehow, in this moment, I felt peace.

A surprising peace washed over me as I approached the farthest cross, tears already streaming down my face. I dipped my hands into the red paint, lifted them to the wood, and pressed them right where I imagined Jesus' hands would have been. I closed my eyes and visualized looking into His eyes. I saw the blood dripping from His thorny crown. I felt His pain—not just physically, but emotionally.

I've been a Christian since I was four, but this moment took everything I'd ever believed and made it real in 3D. The crucifixion was no longer just a story. It became deeply personal.

As the weight of Jesus' deep and unrelenting love hit me, I collapsed to the ground, overwhelmed by the depth of His sacrifice.

And then, something holy happened.

As I lay there, something beyond myself began to unfold—a sacred encounter I never expected. I was suddenly transported in my mind to Luke's deathbed. I saw him take his last breath all over again. A deep wail escaped from my soul—a sound I didn't know I was capable of making. I had cried many times since his passing, but I had never allowed myself to feel my loss this deeply. For the first time, I had space to fully process what had happened—away from my kids, alone with Jesus.

Then something supernatural happened.

My vision continued and I saw Jesus walking toward me, holding a radiant crown—gold, adorned with sparkling, multicolored jewels. He gently wiped my tears, looked into my eyes, and said:

"I am so proud of you. I want you to know—I chose you. Out of all the people in the world, I chose you to be Luke's wife. I chose you to walk beside him, even unto death."

And then, Jesus placed the crown on my head.

That moment changed everything. Before, I had often wondered, Why me? I questioned whether I had done something wrong to deserve this pain. But in an instant, Jesus shifted my perspective. He showed me that it wasn't a punishment—it was a sacred assignment. I had been chosen to be Luke's wife. What a beautiful, holy privilege it was to stand by my husband until the end.

And now, dear friend, I want you to pause for a moment and take that in.

Let it sink deep into your soul: You, too, were chosen.

In your pain, in your suffering, in your questions and confusion—He chose you. Out of the billions of people on this planet, God hand-picked you to be your spouse's partner. You, and no one else, were called to fulfill that role. He trusted you to carry that responsibility, and He is so incredibly proud of you.

And I'm proud of you, too.

You've been through so much. Yet here you are—reading, processing, and working toward healing. That's no small thing. That's strength. That's faith. That's bravery.

After the vision ended, I continued to cry, releasing everything I had been holding in. A retreat leader came and held me, praying over me as I wept. It was one of the most healing moments of my life—finally giving myself permission to surrender to the depth of my grief and let it out.

From that day forward, something shifted. I walked a little lighter. Joy slowly began to return. I felt like God had handed me a gold medal, whispering:

"Well done, my daughter. I see you. I chose you. And I'm proud of you."

And maybe today, He's saying the same thing to you:

"I see you. I chose you. And I'm proud of you." Now take that next brave step, crown held high.

Widow Reflections

1. What changes when you begin to see yourself as chosen by God to be your spouse's partner during their time on earth?

2. When you view your spouses passing through the lens of God's eternal plan, how does that reshape the way you grieve and honor him?

3. Imagine the moment God placed a crown on your head and said, "I chose you." What does that image stir in your heart today?

Widow Action Steps

*Take time this week to write a letter as if God were speaking directly to you. Let Him remind you that you were chosen for your spouse, that He saw your pain, and that He is proud of how you've endured. Let the letter be full of grace, truth, and compassion—something you can return to whenever doubt or grief clouds your view.

*Each morning for the next seven days, look in the mirror and speak this truth aloud: *"I was chosen to be their spouse. I did my best. God sees me, and He is proud."* Speaking it helps it take root in your heart and reframe your grief with purpose and honor.

*Find or create something tangible—a ring, bracelet, crown necklace, or even a simple stone—that reminds you daily: *I was chosen.* Let it be a visible and tactile reminder that God trusted you with a sacred assignment, and that you are walking forward with His blessing.

Goal #27—Embrace Your New Identity

"**I** am the vine; you are the branches. If you remain in me and I in you, you will bear much fruit; apart from me you can do nothing." John 15:5 NIV

Who am I now?

I asked myself as I stared intently at the multiple-choice question on the form: Single, Married, Divorced, Widowed. My heart still whispered married, but with trembling hands, I circled widowed. The next question made tears fill my eyes. Just three words shattered me all over again: Date marriage ended. As if I had a say in that ending.

In an instant, my identity as a wife was replaced with a new, unwanted label: widow. I was no longer Luke's wife. I no longer fit in with the world of couples. It was just... me. And I didn't even know who me was anymore. For nearly 17 years, I had been Luke's wife. That role had become such a core part of who I was. So when it was gone, I felt exposed, unanchored, and completely lost.

Yes, I was still a mother, but deep down, who was I beyond all the roles?

I hated the word widow. Before I became one, I pictured an elderly woman in black with a tight gray bun and cats crawling all over her. Suddenly, that was supposed to be me. A 41-year-old widow. I wasn't ready to be the "cat lady" yet.

Friend, maybe you're asking the same question: Who am I now?

There's no quick answer, but let me share what I've discovered.

I began seeking the truth—not from forms or labels, but from the One who created me. I asked God to show me who I really am. He began whispering reminders: You are loved. You are my daughter. You are redeemed. You are victorious. You are still Mine.

At a recent widow's retreat, I gave each woman a name tag that said "Wife" and asked them to write their wedding date. Tears fell as we honored that identity. Then, I shared my own story—pausing at the moment Luke died—and covered my wife tag with one that read: "Widow - 5/23/20."

One by one, each woman placed her widow tag over her wife tag, and as they did, we cried together. When I came to one of the newest widows, she let out a deep wail—and matched the sound I once made at a grief retreat. I held her in my arms (and sidenote, I am not naturally a hugger—but I am learning to be more comfortable with it!), and I let her weep as long as she needed.

After each woman had her widow tag, I gently reminded them: This is not your full identity. It's a chapter, not your whole story.

Then I invited them to sit with the Lord, listen, and ask: Who do You say I am now?

We turned on soft worship music and spent quiet time listening. One by one, new words began to form: Overcomer. Healer. Brave. Light-bringer.

God gave me two words: Hope Warrior.

He reminded me that my new identity includes carrying hope to others who feel like they're drowning. What is He saying to you?

Yes, you're a widow now. But don't let that be the final word. You are so much more.

A few months after Luke died, I woke up... excited. It was a strange feeling. I realized I had a blank page in front of me in a huge blank book. I could become anyone I wanted. I started to rediscover myself.

I picked up my pen and embraced my identity as a writer—and this book was born.

I signed up for line dancing lessons and embraced my inner line dancer (yes, I bought the cowboy boots).

I made TikToks for widows—even the awkward early ones where I stood on a counter to make a point (yep, you can laugh at @widowgoals).

I bought a paddleboard and became a paddleboarder.

I started a podcast and became a podcaster.

I ran again and became a runner.

I took off my ring, stepped into dating again, and embraced my identity as a single woman.

These new identities didn't erase my grief—but they helped me rediscover my voice.

And through it all, God kept reminding me of the truest part of who I am: who I am in Him.

So, who does God say you are?

Here's a list of truths from Scripture to anchor your identity in Christ. These aren't just comforting words—they are rock-solid promises from your Creator:

Who God Says You Are: Your True Identity in Christ

- You are a child of God – John 1:12

- You are chosen – 1 Peter 2:9

- You are a new creation – 2 Corinthians 5:17

- You are deeply loved – Romans 8:38-39

- You are redeemed – Ephesians 1:7

- You are not alone – Hebrews 13:5

- You are victorious – Romans 8:37

- You are God's masterpiece – Ephesians 2:10

- You are free – Galatians 5:1

- You are a temple of the Holy Spirit – 1 Corinthians 6:19-20

- You are strong in Him – Philippians 4:13

- You are held in God's hand – Isaiah 41:10

- You are an heir with Christ – Romans 8:17

- You are forgiven – 1 John 1:9

- You are seen, known, and called – Jeremiah 1:5

Let these truths settle deep in your soul: You are not forgotten. You are not broken beyond repair. You are not just a widow. You are becoming who God always intended you to be—brave, beautiful, and never alone. He is with you every step of the way.

Widow Reflections

1. What are some labels or roles you've let define you that God may be inviting you to release?

2. What new identity or word is God whispering over your life in this season?

3. Which Bible verse from the list above stands out to you, and why does it resonate with your current journey?

Widow Action Steps

*Spend 15 minutes in quiet reflection with God. Ask Him directly, "Who do You say I am now?" Write down any words, images, or scriptures that come to mind, even if they feel small or unexpected. Return to this often.

*Create a "New Identity" vision board or journal page. Include scripture from the "Who God Says You Are" list, words you feel God is speaking over you, and images that represent who you're becoming. Let this serve as a visual reminder of the hope and purpose ahead.

*Take one bold step to explore a new part of your identity. Sign up for a class, try a hobby, or do something you've always wanted to do—but never did before. Let this act of courage help you rediscover joy and possibility beyond grief.

Goal #28 – Have an Eternal Perspective

"**F**or this world is not our home; we are looking forward to our everlasting home in heaven." – Hebrews 13:14 NLT

Sickness. Suffering. Loss. It's everywhere I look.

I've been deeply burdened by the constant presence of sickness and death all around me. I don't understand the suffering I see—people I care about are struggling physically and emotionally—and I find myself crying out to God, "Why?"

And each time, I hear a gentle whisper in my spirit: "This world is not your home."

It doesn't remove the pain, but those words give me peace—peace in knowing that something far greater awaits us in eternity. One day, we'll be with Jesus. And if our loved ones knew Him too, as I pray they all do, we'll be reunited with them. What a beautiful promise to hold onto.

A few months after Luke died, I attended a grief retreat where something truly supernatural happened. During one of the sessions, the leader invited us to ask Jesus a question:

"I want you to ask Jesus where He was in your most painful moment," she said. "Close your eyes and ask Him."

As peaceful music played in the background, I closed my eyes and was immediately brought back to the morning of Luke's death. But this time, I wasn't reliving it from memory—I was seeing it with spiritual clarity.

The first thing I noticed was our bedroom door. It was closed. That may sound insignificant, but in our home, that door was almost never shut. I didn't remember closing it. Yet in the vision, it was firmly closed, with the long oxygen cord trailing beneath it. I would later learn from Hayden that he had been awake but didn't come in—because the door was shut. God had supernaturally closed it,

Behind that door, I saw the same moments I had lived: Luke's shallow breathing, the urgent call to the hospice nurse, and the stillness before goodbye. I saw myself rushing into the kids rooms again "It's time to say goodbye to Daddy." Waking up Hayley. Her scream rang out again: "No! It's not time!"

But then something shifted.

I was no longer a witness. I was inside the moment—experiencing it as Luke.

I wasn't reliving trauma. I was feeling the peace that he felt in those final minutes. It was unlike anything I had ever known. There was no pain. No fear. Only peace—deep, calm, otherworldly peace.

And then, I began to hear his thoughts.

"I don't have any pain right now. This feels so peaceful."

I heard the voices around me:

"You're the best daddy ever," said Payton.

"You're my best buddy," Hayden whispered.

Hayley sang gently, "You are my sunshine, my only sunshine..."

Luke's mom softly said, "I love you, son."

And then I heard my own voice: "You're going to meet my grandparents today, Luke. And you're going to hear, Well done, my good and faithful servant.'"

In the Prologue, I described how Luke's eyes had turned to the upper corner of the room. I had asked him, "Are you looking at angels?" Now, I saw what he saw: Jesus. Standing there. Glowing. Watching. Waiting.

Then I heard another one of Luke's thoughts: "I'm okay to leave my family."

That thought undid me. I knew how deeply he hated the idea of leaving us. But in that moment, he had been given peace—the kind only God can give.

As "I Can Only Imagine" played, I (as Luke) felt myself rise. I moved toward the light beside Jesus, and the peace that wrapped around me was beyond anything I can describe with earthly language.

And then... the vision ended.

God hadn't just shown me where He was. He showed me what Luke experienced—and that changed everything.

I've shared this vision with many people, and they often tell me it brings them comfort. I know how I wrestled for months, wondering what Luke was thinking and feeling as he died. This vision was a precious gift—one that brought me peace. I believe God gave it to me so I could share it with you. So that you could find peace in knowing your loved one was not alone and was deeply cared for in their final moments.

That vision gave me more than peace—it gave me perspective. It reminded me that this life, with all its heartbreak and beauty, is not the end. It reminded me that everything we're given is a gift.

We come into this world with nothing and leave the same way. Everything we're given in between—our spouses, children, homes, even our time—is a gift. When we embrace this truth, it pulls us back into an eternal perspective.

I once heard it explained like this:

Imagine your life on earth as one inch on a yardstick. Now imagine a ruler extending infinitely beyond what your eyes can see—that's eternity.

We often waste energy on things that don't matter in light of eternity. On those days, I remind myself what truly matters. It's not money, success, or a fancy home—it's fulfilling God's calling on my life.

You might be wondering, "What is God's calling for me?"

If you're newly widowed, your calling may simply be to survive—to breathe, to grieve, and to grow in your faith. As healing comes, God will gently reveal your next steps.

Before Luke died, I was a teacher and entrepreneur. I always found creative ways to earn money. After he died, I took on a few teaching roles to support my family—including a four-month position teaching third grade at the private Christian school my kids attended. The people were wonderful, but something deep inside told me this was no longer my path.

Luke's death changed everything! It gave me a new perspective—and a calling. I knew my mission was now to help widows and to let God make beauty out of the ashes I was handed. That's why I chose to change the entire trajectory of my life.

My calling to minister to others in grief may not be what your calling is. But you can ask God to show you how your life can make an eternal impact.

Because in the end, what truly matters isn't how much we had—but how we loved, how we served, and how we followed God's calling with eternity in mind.

Widow Reflections

1. What would it look like to fully embrace the idea that "this world is not our home"? How might it change the way you approach daily struggles, grief, or the choices you make?

2. In what ways can you see God's gifts in your life, even in the midst of suffering? How can a heart of gratitude shape your perspective on temporary versus eternal things?

3. Are there areas of your life where you might be focusing too much on what is temporary rather than what is eternal? What steps can you take to align your priorities with God's calling for eternal impact?

Widow Action Steps

*Ask God for a glimpse of His eternal perspective. Find a quiet space and invite Jesus into your most painful memory. Close your eyes and ask, "Jesus, where were You?" Write down or journal anything He reveals—it may bring a peace you didn't know you needed.

*Create a gratitude list focused on eternal gifts. Instead of just listing material blessings, try listing things with eternal value—your faith, your growth, the people God has placed in your life, opportunities to serve, etc.

*Identify one area of your life to shift from temporary to eternal focus. Is there something consuming your time, energy, or worry that has no lasting value? Ask God to help you release it. Then, take one step toward something that will leave an eternal impact—maybe encouraging another widow, praying for someone, or sharing your testimony.

Goal #29—Do Something Today to Better Your Future

"**F**or I know the plans I have for you,' declares the Lord, 'plans to prosper you and not to harm you, plans to give you hope and a future.'" – Jeremiah 29:11 NIV

You are still here. You've made it through the hardest days you never imagined you'd face—and you're still standing. That's not small. That's strength. So now, what's next?

Healing isn't just about surviving your past—it's about investing in your future. And you don't have to have it all figured out. You just have to take one step.

Here we are, nearing the end of our time together—but this is just the beginning of your healing journey. So what now? How do we, as the title of this chapter says, better our future?

Every day, I ask myself (and often my 20-year-old son), "What will you do today to better your future?" It's a question that grounds me and reminds me that although I didn't choose this journey, I do have a say in how it unfolds moving forward. You didn't ask for this, and what happened to you is not your fault. But you do have control over your next steps.

Where do you want to be a year from now? Five years from now? And what small step can you take today to get there?

Remember this: a goal that is not written down is just a wish. Do you want to live your life based on wishes, or do you want to live with purpose? Life is partly what happens to you, but more importantly, it's how you respond.

When I think about bettering my future, I look at my life in five main areas: physical, mental, spiritual, relational, and emotional. Each day, I try to do something—no matter how small—in at least one of these areas. Progress doesn't have to be dramatic. It just needs to be consistent.

Physically: Start with One Step

For your body, the simplest thing you can do is walk.

I used to think running was the best way to stay fit. But over time, I've learned that while running has benefits, it can be hard on your joints—especially as we age. Walking, on the other hand, is low-impact, easier on your body, and still provides many of the same cardiovascular benefits.

Research confirms this. A 2013 study published in Arthritis Care & Research confirms that while running burns more calories in less time, it also comes with a higher risk of joint problems like osteoarthritis. Walking is safer for long-term joint health and can be just as effective when done consistently.

Start small: walk 10–15 minutes a day. Walk during work breaks. Park farther from the store. Pace during phone calls. Listen to a podcast (Widowed 2 Soon, anyone?), pray, reflect, or simply breathe in the fresh air. Also, don't forget strength training! Starting around age 30, women lose 3–8% of muscle mass per decade if they are inactive. Lifting weights or doing bodyweight exercises a few times a week can help preserve your strength and energy—something we all need for our widowed journey.

Mentally: Start with Your Mindset

Your mental health affects everything. As a new widow, this is often the area we need to focus on first. If your mind is in a dark place, it's hard to thrive in any other area.

Here are some things that help me:

- Journaling: Set a timer for 5 minutes and write freely. Don't worry about grammar or spelling. Just get your thoughts out—you'll be amazed at the clarity it can bring.

- Set One Small Goal: Instead of a giant to-do list, choose one small, doable goal for the day. Organize a drawer. Make a call. Walk for 15 minutes. And celebrate it—it's a win!

- Practice Gratitude: Yes, you've experienced deep loss. But what do you still have? Your children, your home, your pet, your friends? Make a running list. What we focus on expands. Think about what remains, not only what's missing.

Spiritually: Anchor Your Soul

Grief often shakes our spiritual foundation, but it can also deepen it. Begin your day with a single verse and ask, "What does this mean for me today?" The YouVersion Bible App is a great resource—it sends daily verses and has devotionals for nearly every topic. Spend time in prayer. Ask God for wisdom. Listen to worship music and let it shift the atmosphere of your heart AND in your home. Sit in silence and ask for His peace. He's still with you—closer than ever. God will meet you in ways you've never known before.

Find others who share your faith. Join a Bible study, a church group, or an online community of believers. We were never meant to do life—or grief—alone.

Relationally: Rebuild Connection

As a widow, rebuilding or redefining relationships is essential. Start small: reach out to one person a day. A quick text, a phone call, or extend a coffee invite. These moments remind you that you are not alone and help to strengthen the connections you still have.

And remember: it's okay to set boundaries. If certain relationships drain you or hinder your healing, you can lovingly take a step back. Focus your energy on people who uplift and support you.

Emotionally: Feel It All

I've learned that emotional healing means giving myself permission to feel everything. Grief. Anger. Guilt. Joy. Yes, even joy.

I'll never forget the first time I laughed after Luke died. It surprised me, and immediately, I felt guilty—like I was betraying my grief. But I've since realized that laughter doesn't erase the love or pain. It simply means I'm alive—and healing.

You don't need to have every step mapped out. You just need to take the next right one. Do something today—just one small thing—to better your future. This chapter isn't the end of your story. It's the turning point. The place where you stop surviving and start building again.

You are becoming someone stronger, braver, and wiser than you ever imagined. Your future still holds beauty. And today is the perfect day to begin.

Widow Reflections

1. What is one small step you can take today—physically, mentally, spiritually, relationally, or emotionally—that would help you feel more hopeful about the future?

2. In which area of your life are you currently thriving, and which area needs a little more attention or grace?

3. How can you honor your past while still making room for the possibilities of your future?

Widow Action Steps

*Choose one area of life and commit to one small action today—just one step.

*Write down your short-term and long-term goals and place them where you'll see them.

*Start a "letter to future me"—a vision for where you want to be and how far you've come.

Goal #30 - Live at Peace with God and Everyone

"**A**nd the peace of God, which transcends all understanding, will guard your hearts and your minds in Christ Jesus." Phillipians 4:7 NIV

Peace might feel like a far-off dream right now. Maybe even a word that stings. After everything you've been through, how could peace possibly find you again? You may feel like peace is the last emotion you're experiencing toward God or anyone. Your whole world has been rocked, and you may be angry—at God, at people, and at circumstances you never desired.

But here's the truth: having unrest only hurts you. God wants us to live in peace. He created peace, and it's one of His most precious gifts. This book has been about discovering that peace and learning how to take small steps toward it. In this final chapter, we're going to take a deep dive into what it means to truly live in peace—with God, with others, and within yourself.

If your spouse has just died, I know peace can feel like a distant stranger. The questions, the anger, the "what ifs" and "whys" can leave us feeling anything but peaceful. I went through this several times in my journey.

When Luke was first diagnosed with cancer at age 26—just a few months after our wedding—I was so angry. When the chemo didn't work and he had to have his leg amputated, I was crushed. I couldn't understand why God would give me such an amazing man only to allow him to get sick. I didn't understand then, and I don't understand now. I don't understand why he suffered from cancer, diabetes, pancreatitis, cirrhosis, and so many other things. I still don't understand why he eventually died.

But I have found a way to live at peace—even in the darkest circumstances.

There are still things that try to steal my peace almost daily. I have to make a conscious effort to release them and not dwell on them. Satan knows exactly what to use to provoke me. For me, one of the biggest threats to my peace is rejection.

Over the years, I've had close friends, best friends, even ministry partners walk away from my life without warning. One painful time happened about six months ago. I'll be honest—I let it take me down a dark path.

As we talked about in a previous chapter, our brains often generate ANT's—automatic negative thoughts. When one pops up, your brain will search for more to back it up. If you don't intentionally stop them, they pile up like a snowball, growing bigger and stronger until they threaten to bury you. That's exactly what happened to me.

That one situation brought back every rejection and failure I'd ever experienced. Despite all the education, accomplishments, and encouragement I'd received, I felt defeated and worthless. I now recognize how fiercely the enemy was trying to silence me—trying to derail me from my calling.

It took three whole days of crying, wrestling, and rejecting lies before I let God lift me out of that pit. If I'd continued listening to those lies, I don't think you'd even be holding this book in your hands today.

As I let God heal my heart and remind me of my identity and purpose, I found myself return to a place of peace. The pain didn't vanish, but I released the unrest. I surrendered the rejection. And I trusted that God still has a plan—even when it hurts.

One phrase from a sermon years ago has stayed with me: "If God allowed it, I can accept it."

God did not cause your spouse's death—but He did allow it. We live in a broken, fallen world where pain, loss, and death are real. While we may never like what's happened, we do get to choose how we respond. That phrase has helped me again and again in situations I never thought I could accept.

And here's something else that really blew my mind: I recently learned at church that it's scientifically impossible to feel anxiety and thankfulness at the same time. I was so intrigued that I went home and investigated it. Sure enough, research supports this! When you experience gratitude, your brain activates regions associated with emotional regulation and peace—like the prefrontal cortex—while decreasing activity in the amygdala, the part of your brain that processes fear and anxiety.

In other words, gratitude shifts your brain away from stress and toward peace.

So now, when I feel anxiety creeping in, I practice gratitude in real time. I speak it out loud, write it down, or simply thank God for breath in my lungs. It changes something inside me. It creates space for peace.

I've worked hard to cultivate gratitude in every season. And I know—being thankful after your spouse dies might sound impossible. But what's the alternative? Living a life full of bitterness, anger, and resentment?

Over the past four years of working closely with widows, I've witnessed a wide range of responses to loss. Two people can face similar tragedies and respond in completely different ways. One finds peace and begins to thrive. The other remains stuck in deep grief.

Why? I believe the difference is peace.

I'm not talking about generic, surface-level peace. I'm talking about that peace that passes all understanding. The kind you can't explain. The kind that anchors your soul even when life makes no sense.

That kind of peace? It comes from Jesus.

Yes, you might find moments of calm outside of Him—but the deep, soul-level, I-will-be-okay-no-matter-what peace? That's from Him alone.

Peace has been one of the greatest gifts I've ever received—and the best part is, it's not just for me. It's for you. It's unlimited. And it's free.

What does peace feel like?

Peace feels like freedom.

Peace feels like lightness.

Peace feels like trusting God in the middle of the storm.

Peace feels like sitting on your Heavenly Father's lap, wrapped in the safest embrace you've ever known.

Peace is knowing that no matter what comes next—He's got you.

He will cover you with the peace that passes all understanding.

If there's one thing I want you to take away from this chapter—and really, from this entire book—it's this: peace is possible, even in our most broken state. Even after the unthinkable. Even when your heart is shattered and your future looks nothing like you planned.

I won't pretend it's easy. I know what it's like to feel angry, confused, rejected, and just plain tired of everything. But I also know what it's like to invite God into that mess and watch Him do what only He can do. He brings peace—not just to your circumstances, but deep into your soul.

Living at peace with God, with others, and with yourself is a choice you'll have to make over and over again. Some days, you'll get it right. Other days, the thoughts will swirl and the wounds will ache—but friend, you'll remember what's true. You'll remember who you are, whose you are, and that peace is a gift you can receive again and again.

You're not alone in this—I see you, and I've been you. And I promise: peace is not just a wish. It's already being offered by the One who holds your heart. All you have to do is open your hands and receive it.

Widow Reflections

1. Where in my life do I still feel unrest—with God, with others, or with myself—and what might be keeping me from peace?

2. What has helped me experience peace in the past, and how can I intentionally return to that space when I feel overwhelmed?

3. How has rejection or grief affected my ability to receive peace, and what would it look like to surrender that pain to God today?

Widow Action Steps

*List three things you're thankful for each day this week. Gratitude isn't just a feeling—it's a practice that rewires your brain and invites peace.

*Pray this simple prayer each morning:"God, help me live at peace with You, with others, and within myself today."

*Reach out to someone you need to make peace with—or release it silently in your heart. You can't control their response, but you can choose peace for yourself.

Final Thoughts

As we come to the close of this journey together, my prayer for you is simple yet profound: that you leave these pages knowing, deep in your soul, just how deeply God loves you. His love is not distant or conditional—it is personal, powerful, and healing. He sees every tear, understands every ache, and walks with you every single step of the way.

I hope that through these words, you've gathered not just inspiration, but real, practical tools to support you on your healing journey. May you feel more equipped to face each day with strength, hope, and courage. Healing isn't a straight line, and it doesn't happen overnight—but you now carry with you wisdom, insight, and the reassurance that progress is always possible.

More than anything, I want you to remember this: you are not alone. Even in your loneliest moments, there is a community of others walking a similar path—people who understand, who care, and who stand with you. And above all, the God who formed you and loves you is always near, inviting you into deeper healing, greater hope, and a life that still holds beauty and purpose.

You are seen. You are loved. You are never, ever alone.

Love Always,

Michelle Bader Ebersole

Frequently asked Questions About Widowhood

One of the most common questions I hear from widows is: "*Am I doing this right?*" And I get it. Grief doesn't come with a rulebook. We're just trying to survive something we never wanted to be a part of. Over the years, I've heard many of the same questions—ones I've asked myself too. So, I want to answer some of those frequently asked questions and remind you: *you're not alone, and there's no wrong way to grieve.*

1. When will my life return to normal?

The short answer? It won't. But that doesn't mean your life can't be beautiful again.

There's no "going back" to who you were before the loss. But there is a *moving forward*—into something new. This new version of life might feel foreign and uncomfortable at first. But over time, it can become meaningful, joyful, and even full of purpose again.

Many widows resist the phrase *"new normal"* because it feels like letting go of the life they loved. But embracing what *is* doesn't mean forgetting what *was*. You can carry your memories and love with you while still stepping into something new. That might look like rediscovering old passions, starting fresh routines, or even welcoming new relationships. Let go of comparison, and allow yourself to see what's still possible.

2. When should I take off my wedding ring?

This is one of the most personal decisions you'll ever make. And the only timeline that matters is yours.

Some widows remove their rings right away. Others never do. I took mine off at the one-year mark because I knew in my heart I was ready to be open to dating again. But that was *my* story. Yours might look completely different—and that's okay.

If you're not ready, that's fine. If you find comfort in wearing it, keep it on. If it feels heavy, you can transition it into something else—like a necklace, a new piece of jewelry, or a keepsake in a memory box. Taking it off doesn't erase the love you shared. It simply marks a shift in your journey.

3. When should I go through their belongings?

There is no "right"time—only your time.

Some widows clean everything out quickly. Others leave things untouched for years. My advice? If you're unsure, don't rush. Box things up. Store them. Give yourself space to decide later. I've talked to so many widows who said, "*I wish I hadn't gotten rid of that so soon.*"

This process can feel sacred and painful all at once. You might want help from a friend or prefer to do it alone. You may cry, laugh, or feel numb. All of that is normal. Keep the items that carry meaning. You don't have to decide what to do with them right away. Healing happens at your pace.

4. Do I have to go through all the stages of grief?

You've probably heard of the five stages—denial, anger, bargaining, depression, acceptance. But here's the thing: grief is not a checklist.

Those "stages" were actually created to describe the experience of *dying*, not grieving. And while they can be helpful for understanding emotions, real-life grief is way messier. It comes in waves.

Some days you're doing okay, and the next a smell, a memory, or a song knocks the wind out of you.

That's normal. That's grief. Give yourself grace. This is your journey.

5. When will the pain go away?

The pain doesn't fully go away—but it does change.

In the beginning, it's all-consuming. But with time and healing, it softens. One day, you'll notice that you smiled and meant it. That laughter didn't feel like a betrayal. That joy is possible again.

The goal isn't to stop missing your spouse—it's to learn how to live with the loss in a way that allows room for light. You'll always carry the love, but you don't have to carry the weight the same way forever.

6. Why am I grieving so many things from my past?

This happened to me—after Luke died, I suddenly found myself grieving other hurts from my past, even ones I had buried since childhood. I didn't understand why it was all coming up at once until my grief counselor explained it using a powerful image. She said grief is like a stew—when you're grieving, everything you've ever grieved can rise to the surface. That explanation helped me make sense of the overwhelming emotions I was experiencing. It wasn't just about Luke—it was a lifetime of pain bubbling up, asking to be seen and healed.

7. How do I know when I'm ready to date again?

If the thought of dating makes you physically ill, you're not ready. But if there's even a *tiny* spark of curiosity or hope, you might be closer than you think.

There's no set timeline. Don't let guilt hold you back—loving again doesn't erase your first love. Your heart is capable of more love, not less. Grief and new beginnings can exist together.

When you do decide to date (if you do), go at your own pace. There's no pressure to make anything happen quickly. Trust your gut, and remember: this is your story to write.

8. How long will I grieve?
The honest answer? Likely forever. But it won't always feel this heavy.

Grief becomes part of you, but it won't always define you. With time, it softens. It grows quieter. You'll learn how to carry it differently. It will shape who you are—but it doesn't get the final say in your story.

9. What if people judge me for moving forward?
They probably will. Let them.

Some people think you're moving on *too fast*. Others will say you're *stuck in the past*. The truth? You could do everything "right" and still face judgment.

The only voice that matters is your own—and God's. This is *your* journey. You get to decide what healing looks like.

10. Is it okay that I still miss them, even when I'm laughing or enjoying life?

Yes. Missing someone and finding joy again are not opposites—they can exist in the same moment. Grief doesn't cancel out joy, and joy doesn't erase grief.
Your love was real, and your loss is real. But so is your capacity for life, laughter, and hope.
You don't need to feel guilty for living again. In fact, your healing honors your love. Let joy in, one moment at a time, without apology.

Acknowledgements

First and most importantly I want to thank Jesus for getting me through my darkest season. He carried me through the valley of grief and gave me the strength, courage, and words to keep going. Every page of *Widow Goals* is a testimony of His faithfulness.

To my late husband, Luke — thank you for the love we shared, the life we built, and the legacy you left behind. You will always be part of my story. Writing this book was part of my healing and a way to honor you.

To my husband, Joel — thank you for loving me through my grief, for encouraging me to keep writing, and for standing by my side as I stepped into a new season. Your love has been a gift I never expected but deeply cherish.

To my children — Hayden, Hayley, and Payton — you are my greatest blessings. Thank you for your patience during the countless hours I spent writing, for your love when I needed strength, and for your resilience as we've journeyed through grief together.

To my parents, Steve and Karen Rommel — thank you for always believing in me and helping me know I could achieve anything I set my mind to. Your unwavering support through Luke's illness and death meant the world to me and I don't think I would have survived without you.

To my brothers and their wives, Abe and Amy Rommel, and Nathan and Jessica Rommel— I don't know if I would have survived the last five years without your support, love, and help with the kids. Thank you for always being there and walking beside me through my hardest season.

To **Angela Heitz** — thank you for lovingly editing this entire book as a fellow widow who truly understands the heart behind every word. Your wisdom, time, and care made this book better than I could have imagined.

To **Patty Gallegos Day**— my writing partner, fellow widow and constant encourager. Thank you for believing in this book and in me from the very beginning and reading my first chapters and cheering me on!

To **Stacie Campbell Waits and Jessica Winters** — you were the first widows who poured into me, and told me it *would* get better. Your friendship, honesty, and all the fun moments we've shared have brought so much joy to my life.

To **Melissa Sutton** — thank you for being such a thoughtful and loyal friend, always remembering the hard days and showing up with love.

To **my best friend Deborah Johnston** —You were there the day Luke died, and you've never stopped supporting me. I'll never forget that. Thanks for all the fun memories since we were 18!

To **my counselor, Kathleen Sawyer-** thank you for walking with me through the depths of grief with such wisdom and compassion. So many of the principles you shared have made their way into this book. Your support helped me heal, grow, and find clarity. I'm deeply grateful.

To **all my widow friends** — thank you for sharing your hearts, your stories, your tears, and your strength. I wrote this for you, with you in mind. May it remind you that you are never alone.

To **my launch team, ARC readers, and the *Widowed 2 Soon* community** — your encouragement, feedback, and prayers made this book possible. Thank you for championing it into the world.

And to every widow who feels lost in grief — this book is for you. You are seen. You are loved. And you are never without hope.

About the Author

Michelle Bader Ebersole is an author, speaker, podcast host, and founder of *Widow Goals*, a nonprofit organization committed to helping widows not only survive—but thrive. After losing her husband Luke in 2020, Michelle found herself navigating the uncharted waters of grief while raising their three children. Through the pain, she discovered a powerful calling: to walk alongside other widows and offer real hope, practical tools, and the reminder that they are not alone.

Drawing from her personal journey of loss and healing, Michelle created *Widow Goals: Steps to Finding Peace When You Lose Your Spouse*, a heartfelt guide filled with faith, wisdom, and encouragement. She also hosts the *Widowed 2 Soon* podcast, where she shares raw, honest conversations with other widows and widowers about grief, faith, and rebuilding life after loss.

Michelle's work reaches thousands of grieving hearts each month through her podcast, speaking engagements, social media, and a growing network of over 30 Widow Goals support groups worldwide. She is passionate about helping others rediscover joy, find their purpose, and live with eternal perspective.

Michelle lives in Ridgefield, Washington, with her husband Joel and her three teenagers. When she's not writing or speaking, she loves spending time with family, line dancing, paddle boarding, exploring, and laughing with friends. Her greatest joy is seeing God turn her pain into purpose and watching others do the same.

Connect with Michelle: Website, podcast, Widow Facebook Community, PDF What Not To Say and more!

Michelle would love to hear from you, you can email her at **michelle@widowgoals.org**

I Would Love Your Help!

Dear Reader,

Thank you so much for reading *Widow Goals: Steps to Finding Peace When You Lose Your Spouse.* I pray this book brought comfort, encouragement, and hope as you navigate your own grief journey.

If this book impacted you in any way, would you consider leaving a brief review? Your words—just a few sentences—can help another widow find this book at just the right time.

You don't need to write anything long or fancy—just share how this book helped you. Your voice matters more than you know.

How to Leave a Review on Amazon:

1. Log into your Amazon account.

2. Go to the *Widow Goals: Steps to Finding Peace When You Lose Your Spouse* book page.

3. Select the number of stars you'd like to rate the book.

4. Write your review in the "Customer Reviews" section.

5. Click **Submit**.

6. Or simply scan or tap the QR code below to go straight to the review page:

How to Leave a Barnes & Noble Review

Here's how to leave a review:

1. **Go to the Barnes & Noble website**
   Visit: www.barnesandnoble.com

2. **Search for the book**
   Type **Widow Goals by Michelle Bader Ebersole** in the search bar and click on the book cover to open the product page.

3. **Scroll down to the "Customer Reviews" section**
   You'll see a spot where you can rate the book and share your thoughts.

4. **Click "Write a Review"**

   ○ Choose your star rating

   ○ Add a title and write your review

   ○ Submit!

Thank you for being part of this mission to help widows not only survive, but thrive.

With gratitude,

Michelle Bader Ebersole

www.ingramcontent.com/pod-product-compliance
Lightning Source LLC
Chambersburg PA
CBHW071732120626
46550CB00002B/487